Ashram Notes

BY THE ASCENDED MASTER

El Morya

DICTATED TO
HIS AMANUENSIS

Mark L. Prophet

1952 – 1958

EDITED AND COMPILED BY

Elizabeth Clare Prophet

Ashram Notes
BY THE ASCENDED MASTER
El Morya

DICTATED TO HIS AMANUENSIS
Mark L. Prophet
1952 - 1958
EDITED AND COMPILED BY
Elizabeth Clare Prophet

Published by
The Summit Lighthouse®

LIBRARY OF CONGRESS CATALOG CARD NUMBER: 89-62294

INTERNATIONAL STANDARD BOOK NUMBER: 0-922729-02-6

Printed in the United States of America

Facing page: The Ascended Master El Morya

The Chart of Your Divine Self

There are three figures represented in the Chart, which we will refer to as the upper figure, the middle figure, and the lower figure.

The upper figure is the I AM Presence, the I AM THAT I AM, the individualization of God's presence for every son and daughter of the Most High.

The Divine Monad consists of the I AM Presence surrounded by the spheres (color rings) of light that comprise the Causal Body. This is the body of First Cause that contains within it man's "treasure laid up in heaven"—words and works, thoughts and feelings of virtue, attainment, and light—pure energies of love that have risen from the plane of action in time and space as the result of man's judicious exercise of free will and his harmonious qualification of the stream of life that issues forth from the heart of the Presence and descends to the level of the Christ Self, thence to invigorate and enliven the embodied soul.

The middle figure in the Chart is the Mediator between God and man, called the Holy Christ Self, the Real Self, or the Christ consciousness. It has also been referred to as the Higher Mental Body or one's Higher Consciousness.

This Inner Teacher overshadows the lower self, which consists of the soul evolving through the four planes of Matter using the vehicles of the four lower bodies (the etheric, or memory, body; the mental body; the emotional, or desire, body; and the physical body) to balance karma and fulfill the divine plan.

Mark L. Prophet

The three figures of the Chart correspond to the Trinity of Father (the upper figure), Son (the middle figure), and Holy Spirit (the lower figure). The latter is the intended temple of the Holy Spirit, whose sacred fire is indicated in the enfolding violet flame. The lower figure corresponds to you as a disciple on the Path. Your soul is the nonpermanent aspect of being, which is made permanent through the ritual of the ascension.

The ascension is the process whereby the soul, having balanced her karma and fulfilled her divine plan, merges first with the Christ consciousness and then with the living Presence of the I AM THAT I AM. Once the ascension has taken place, the soul, the nonpermanent aspect of being, becomes the Incorruptible One, a permanent atom in the Body of God. The Chart of Your Divine Self is therefore a diagram of yourself—past, present, and future.

The lower figure represents the son of man or child of the Light evolving beneath his own 'Tree of Life'. This is how you should visualize yourself standing in the violet flame, which you invoke daily in the name of the I AM Presence and your Holy Christ Self in order to purify your four lower bodies in preparation for the ritual of the alchemical marriage—your soul's union with the Beloved, your Holy Christ Self.

The lower figure is surrounded by a tube of light, which is projected from the heart of the I AM Presence in answer to your call. It is a cylinder of white light that sustains a forcefield of protection 24 hours a day, so long as you guard it in harmony. It is also invoked daily with the "Heart, Head and Hand Decrees" and may be reinforced as needed.

The threefold flame of Life is the divine spark sent from the I AM Presence as the gift of life,

THE CHART OF YOUR DIVINE SELF

consciousness, and free will. It is sealed in the secret chamber of the heart that through the Love, Wisdom and Power of the Godhead anchored therein the soul may fulfill her reason for being in the physical plane. Also called the Christ flame and the liberty flame, or fleur-de-lis, it is the spark of a man's Divinity, his potential for Christhood.

The silver (or crystal) cord is the stream of life, or "lifestream," that descends from the heart of the I AM Presence to the Holy Christ Self to nourish and sustain (through the chakras) the soul and its vehicles of expression in time and space. It is over this 'umbilical' cord that the energy of the Presence flows, entering the being of man at the crown and giving impetus for the pulsation of the threefold flame as well as the physical heartbeat.

When a round of the soul's incarnation in Matter-form is finished, the I AM Presence withdraws the silver cord, whereupon the threefold flame returns to the level of the Christ, and the soul clothed in the etheric garment gravitates to the highest level of her attainment where she is schooled between embodiments until her final incarnation when the great law decrees she shall go out no more.

The dove of the Holy Spirit descending from the heart of the Father is shown just above the head of the Christ. When the son of man puts on and becomes the Christ consciousness as Jesus did, he merges with the Holy Christ Self. The Holy Spirit is upon him and the words of the Father, the beloved I AM Presence, are spoken, "This is my beloved Son in whom I AM well pleased" (Matt. 3:17).

A more detailed explanation of the Chart of Your Divine Self is given in *The Lost Teachings of Jesus* and *Climb the Highest Mountain* by Mark L. Prophet and Elizabeth Clare Prophet.

Contents

A Word
about
THE ASHRAM

---

by Mark L. Prophet

Just as the moments of life woven into the fleeting garment of time contain mundane impulses, so there are divine pulsations that sustain all worlds, whether visible or invisible.

Man can attune with these divine pulsations here and now to alter the quality of the garment of time that he weaves. In this manner he will insure his admission to the Ashram and through the portals of its fellowship enter the company of those immortal masters of the ages whose victory over self and circumstance raised them to the ascended state in the heavenly kingdom.

Your attunement with the higher octaves today can be even more effective because the Ascended Masters are devoting themselves in an extraordinary service to life. This service enables all who work hand in hand with them to victoriously outpicture the pattern eternal, a pattern that God intends for every man and woman on earth. For this reason and to this end was the Ashram founded.

In every era, only the few have attained to divine mastery through the Christ consciousness and earned "inscribement" by angelic pen on the scroll of the immortal Brotherhood. Today these all-wise and loving beings are giving of their own hard-won freedom and momentum of mastery to assist the unawakened and unascended of God's children who, though caught in the web of their dense creation, are willing to put forth the effort to be free.

The cries of world pain and distress have reached the ears of angelic watchers sent by the Creator to silently observe and report to cosmic councils the affairs of a world caught in the net of atomic matter and error-generated conflict. In accordance with divine law, these masterful beings see to it that the calls from earth are answered in God's own way.

The Ashram of Morya El is one answer to the call of unascended lifestreams who desire to reduce world suffering and serve the cause of world awakening. It carries a message full of hope to brothers small and great on earth. It opens a door that no man can shut and establishes a shining pathway for souls to reach up beyond the seemingly silent veil into the realm of pure Love. Here the care of the one Father is manifest for all of his children, who were created to inherit the blessings of his kingdom.

Beyond the confines of race and the conflict of creed, the Ashram parts the veil so that the soul may commune with divinely ordained master teachers who will show her how freedom in the highest and most complete sense of the word can be the lot of everyone.

Devotees of the Light around the world have banded together in the Ashram to unite in service to help their brethren overcome obstacles such as time, space, caste or their life's calling that may prevent them from knowing one another and serving together. By the strength of their spiritual union, the Ashram devotees desire to be the Brotherhood's link to those earnest souls on earth who must yet find the way to the abode of the Masters.

By uniting the energies of the students and chelas (disciples) with those of the Masters of Wisdom, the Ashram will establish focal points for transmitting the higher impulses of the Masters' blessings into the thinking and feeling worlds of mankind and Nature, thus changing the path of thorns to one of beauty.

The ascended and unascended beings who sponsor this harmonizing activity at inner levels yearn to see all people's lives lit by the torch of freedom, which bears heaven's comfort to earth. They seek to establish a worldwide communion of embodied devotees and Ascended Masters that may ultimately result in many souls reuniting with God through the ritual of the ascension.

The sponsoring Master of the Ashram, the Ascended Master Morya El, will endeavor to gradually unfold in the mind and heart of each student the tested and proven methods of meditation and the tremendous power of invocation to God when correctly used. Through each student's God Presence the Master will assist in bringing to him—and through him to the world—the benefits and glory of Light's radiation from the heavenly gates now ajar.

As the students of the Ashram engage in such activities as the Master shall direct, they will note gentle changes that bring peace into their personal lives as well as into the lives of all who are touched by their reaching out. Our calls for Light will not go unheeded. They will enable the Light-evolutions of our earth to finally send forth the beautiful beams of pure Light and Love as God intended them to do.

The Ashram is not a mere social outlet for the ego to strut about and exploit its fellowmen; on the contrary, it exists to open opportunities for real and transcendent service to the Brotherhood for the aspiring soul who is not content to drift with the tides of life without moorings.

No personality is glorified at the human level in the Ashram program, which seeks only to exemplify the Ascended Master way of life and to magnify the Lord Christ in our members. We ask neither fees nor dues and encourage you to choose in God freedom whatever religion or mystical path you will walk in, so long as you walk in the Light of your God Presence.

But we do ask you to learn the meaning of trustworthiness and the motto of the Brotherhood: To Know, to Dare, to Do and to Be Silent. For, concerning the mysteries of the kingdom, Jesus said to his disciples, "Give not that which is holy unto the dogs, neither cast ye your pearls before swine, lest they trample them under their feet, and turn again and rend you."

Our methods are simple and they are dedicated to a sublime purpose: the expansion of your soul-light and service to humanity. Let the Light from your God Presence be your guide and let time bring forth its proof.

You can accomplish the expansion of your soul-light through the application of the teaching contained in our Ashram Notes, which are letters from our founder, El Morya, and other Ascended Masters of the Great White Brotherhood. You may choose to keep these in a notebook for further study. As your understanding grows, their value to you will grow also.

You can render your world service by participating in meditation periods that are observed simultaneously by our members. Dictated by El Morya and sponsored from on high, these rituals will increase the Good radiating through you to our sweet earth.

It is to this opportunity that we who serve in the Ashram call you. We invite you to take part in rendering a service to life that will free by love countless millions of our brothers and sisters who endlessly tread the wheel of karma. So often these "know not what they do," but live blindly, without hope, as if cast into a pit of despair.

If you join in these rituals, you will tune in with singleness of purpose to the great radiations of the Ascended Masters and those of your brothers and sisters on every continent.

In the Ashram, we work to rebuild our lives according to the pattern directed to us from our own individualized God Presence and Holy Christ Self. We inwardly pledge to work for a divine renaissance on earth. And we daily rebuild the inner temple according to the pattern we individually receive from God in our meditations on the mount of illumination.

Thus we pray that with our lives and efforts it will be possible to create once again a "new heaven and a new earth." We look to set an example and to guide souls of Light into the permanent golden age, when the Ascended Masters restore their earthly ashrams and once again move freely in the physical octave to bless the embodied children of God with their visible presence.

May the new era come quickly and rest upon our blessed earth and her people forever. And may our humble offering increase the rainbow rays of our Causal Bodies to a magnitude that will assist many to return Home together to the heart of the Father.

The Covenant of the Magi
by El Morya

Father, into thy hands I commend my being. Take me and use me—my efforts, my thoughts, my resources, all that I AM—in thy service to the world of men and to thy noble cosmic purposes, yet unknown to my mind.

Teach me to be kind in the way of the Law that awakens men and guides them to the shores of Reality, to the confluence of the River of Life, to the Edenic source, that I may understand that the leaves of the Tree of Life, given to me each day, are for the healing of the nations; that as I garner them into the treasury of being and offer the fruit of my loving adoration to Thee and to thy purposes supreme, I shall indeed hold covenant with Thee as my guide, my guardian, my friend.

For Thou art the directing connector who shall establish my lifestream with those heavenly contacts, limited only by the flow of the hours, who will assist me to perform in the world of men the most meaningful aspect of my individual life plan as conceived by Thee and executed in thy name by the Karmic Board of spiritual overseers who, under thy holy direction, do administer thy laws.

So be it, O eternal Father, and may the covenant of thy beloved Son, the living Christ, the Only Begotten of the Light, teach me to be aware that he liveth today within the tri-unity of my being as the Great Mediator between my individualized Divine Presence and my human self; that he raiseth me into Christ consciousness and thy divine realization in order that as the eternal Son becomes one with the Father, so I may ultimately become one with Thee in that dynamic moment when out of union is born my perfect freedom to move, to think, to create, to design, to fulfill, to inhabit, to inherit, to dwell and to be wholly within the fullness of thy Light.

Father, into thy hands I commend my being.

Ashram Notes

Greetings, Dear One—

As you are God's child, it is my privilege to welcome you to the Ashram. Dedicated to God, the Ashram is built in his cosmic consciousness; and it is our aim, even as it is your aim, to dwell always in the Ashramic consciousness. May our minds dwell eternally in the Light of his wisdom and presence.

Our advices and blessings shall come to you outwardly in this format. Inwardly God knoweth and thou knowest. And He who is within you shall give you peace, power and love as you engage your spirits in our group meditations.

We offer "The Unison Ritual" at our bimonthly meditation meetings that take place at our respective locations the first and third Sundays of each month at 9:30 p.m. MST.

We offer daily at sunrise and sunset the "Great Central Sun Ritual," which you may choose to observe at sunrise or sunset your time or at any time you feel moved to give adoration to the Sun.

We participate daily at 9:00 a.m. or 9:00 p.m. MST in the "Ritual for Attunement with God's Holy Will." The rituals for these three meditations are attached.

If adjusting the times of your bimonthly and daily meditations to ours is inconvenient, please feel free to schedule them at the time that is best for you and your group.

Whatever time you are able to come together, be assured that your heart's offering will greatly benefit the planetary evolution. It is best if you can synchronize with us; but if this is not possible, be sure to keep your bimonthly meditations at the same hour so as to establish a regular, rhythmic offering to the cosmos.

From the clouds of God...

May there now pour out upon your soul and consciousness a celestial flood of harmony.

May there pour out upon you peace.

May there pour out upon you contact with Hierarchy.

May you be a channel who, with other willing servers, serves many hearts, even the little child that shall lead them.

May you be a channel who can with joy give a cup of cold water in Christ's name.

And through your service and love may all humanity be blessed.

We of the Ashram salute you, O child of the Divine!

Eternal blessings,

1

The Unison Ritual
(First and Third Sundays 9:30 p.m. MST)

I

I AM Thy Holy Love!

I AM Thy Secret Love Star!

Before Thy Holy Love and before Thy Secret Love Star, O Father of Lights—with whom there is no variableness, neither shadow of turning—I bow.

Show me thy pure river of water of Life, clear as crystal, proceeding out of the throne of God and of the Lamb. Let thy Life, Light and Consciousness flow through my crystal cord as the crystal pure river that proceeds from the throne of thy Blessed I AM Presence and Holy Christ Self with me.

O Thou Lamb of God, take me to thy heart, receive my soul as thy bride. Thou who art worthy, open the seven seals of my Book of Life.

Blessing and honour and glory and power be unto him that sitteth upon the throne and unto the Lamb for ever and ever!

Open my seven chakras, that I might transmit thy Light for the building of the antahkarana* between all Light-bearers of this world and cosmos.

*antahkarana [Sanskrit, "internal sense organ"]: the web of life; the net of light spanning Spirit and Matter connecting and sensitizing the whole of creation within itself and to the heart of God.

Reveal to me the wonder of the Woman clothed with the Sun and her Divine Manchild!

Reveal to me my Divine Father and my Divine Mother, Alpha and Omega!

Thy will be done on earth as it is in heaven!

O dearest LORD God of all who have descended from the Word, which was with Brahman in the Beginning, make me one with Thee in the Ending of cycles in this Matter Cosmos even as I was one with Thee in the Beginning of cycles.

Radiate through me thy Love, my Love: to all who stand before the throne of God and before the Lamb, clothed with white robes and palms in their hands; to the entire Spirit of the Great White Brotherhood, of which I AM a part; and to the angels and the Twenty-four Elders and the Four Beasts—the Lion, the Calf, the Man and the Flying Eagle—who worship God before his throne.

By this, "The Unison Ritual," make all members of the Ashram one, as Above, so below, as we recite together saying,

Amen: Blessing and glory and wisdom and thanksgiving and honour and power and might be unto our God forever and ever! OM

O dearest LORD God, allow us also to come out of the great tribulation of personal and planetary karma; and allow us also to wash our robes in the sacred fire and the violet flame and to make them white in the blood of the Lamb.

And when our soul's journey is through, dearest LORD, allow us to be with the saints and hierarchies serving God day and night in his temple in the Great Central Sun. And may our Father of Lights, Lord

Sanat Kumara, who has saved our souls through the Son of God Jesus Christ, dwell among us and we with him forevermore.

Beloved Mighty I AM Presence, radiate through us thy Love, our Love, to all of thy children who are lost in the shadows. Quicken their heart flames through thy Holy Love and thy Secret Love Star, whose Light is released now through our chakras, that they may come alive again and be made Sons of God through the Sacred Heart of Jesus Christ and the Immaculate Heart of the Blessed Virgin Mary.

O LORD my God

I AM Thy Holy Love!

I AM Thy Secret Love Star!

II

Instruction:

Engage in a period of meditation, centering your attention in your heart. Visualize the Sacred Heart of Jesus superimposed over your own, alternating this thoughtform with that of the Immaculate Heart of Mother Mary and the Diamond Heart of El Morya. In addition, see yourself and the members of El Morya's Ashram, as well as all Lightbearers of this world and cosmos, enfolded in their Holy Christ Self. Then visualize and send a strong ray of Light from your heart to theirs. See and feel this powerful beacon, its needlelike rays connecting you with all hearts of Light, establishing the antahkarana you have called forth through the Sacred Heart of Jesus, the Immaculate Heart of Mother Mary and the Diamond Heart of El Morya.

Day and night keep the picture in your mind of a cosmic antahkarana connecting the unascended with the ascended Light-bearers, all of whom together, as Above, so below, compose the entire Spirit of the Great White Brotherhood.

Call to your Mighty I AM Presence that the Light invoked through all affirmations, mantrams, prayers and decrees be sealed in a reservoir of Love to be directed by the Cosmic Christ wherever it is needed to heal, strengthen and unite the Light-bearers. Then give the following invocation while visualizing the Master Jesus Christ overshadowed by the Cosmic Christ:

O Radiant One, Thou Saviour, Thou Cosmic Christ—supreme in Divine Pity, supreme in Divine Compassion, supreme before the kingdom of Archangels and angels and the powers of Elohim—make of us one Mystical Body of the Cosmic Christ, we who aspire to be one in the Ashramic consciousness, one in a crystal chalice of thy Divine Will. Turn our wills to Thee as we recite in unison the "Prayer of Saint Francis."

Prayer of Saint Francis

Lord,
> Make me an instrument of thy peace.
> Where there is hatred let me sow love;
> Where there is injury, pardon;
> Where there is doubt, faith;
> Where there is despair, hope;
> Where there is darkness, light; and
> Where there is sadness, joy.

O Divine Master,
> Grant that I may not so much
> Seek to be consoled as to console;
> To be understood as to understand;
> To be loved as to love.
> For it is in giving that we receive,
> It is in pardoning that we are pardoned, and
> It is in dying that we are born to eternal Life.

May the seamless garment of the Holy Christ Self enfold us, each one, and all of the children of the Father-Mother God, raising us in peace profound to the cross of Light.

I AM standing in the vortex of a radiating aura of thanksgiving to Life. I AM sending forth gratitude to my God, who is Life, for living and for giving me a portion of his God Flame sealed in the heart of my Being.

Through the ever-widening circles of this aura of thanksgiving, I AM reaching everyone in El Morya's worldwide Ashram who is offering this invocation in unison as we radiate Light to one another, heart to heart, God Flame to God Flame, worlds without end.

And I AM ascending evermore to Thee, like sweet incense, with the members of the Ashram and the ascended host, O Thou the All Good!

I AM radiating Light! Light! Light! in the Spirit of the Cosmic Christ! I AM sending forth Divine Love, Wisdom and Power to all servants of God!

I AM invoking my beloved friends the Seven Archangels and the hosts of Light to raise up co-workers in our Ashram for God and to protect and strengthen us in his service. Cut us free! Cut us free! Cut us free!

I AM merging now the Light from my very own God Presence and Holy Christ Self with the ministering angels of the sacred fire of God and with all who hold sacred the "communion of the saints" within the precincts of our Ashram.

I AM merging now my mind and heart and spirit with the Cosmic Christ and the divine Masters, Jesus Christ, Mother Mary, Saint Germain and El Morya. And especially do I now submit and subordinate my soul to the blessed Holy Will of my eternal Father-Mother God.

As the instrument of the Holy One of God, I AM directing Life, Light, Truth and Love, wise-dominion, strength, energy and health everywhere it is needed, to each part of Life that is devoted to the Triune God.

I AM concentrating all the Power, Wisdom and Love of my God-free being in the secret chamber of my heart and I AM sending forth at this moment in eternity (in a concerted action with my brothers and sisters on earth and in heaven) the Light of the Trinity from my God Presence and Holy Christ Self to all chelas of the Will of God, worlds without end.

Let the full Power, Wisdom and Love of the Trinity *sweep! sweep! sweep!* and *sweep!* through the earth to release to all life that is God in manifestation the pattern of God's beautiful Love and Perfection from the Central Sun-Source of creation.

Beloved God Presence, I call to you now to awaken all hearts of children of the Light everywhere to this beautiful Love and Perfection that the Father-Mother God have sealed in their original seed of Life for the full flowering of their souls unto thy glory and their reunion with Thee.

Awaken in them the memory of their Divine Parents, of their spiritual nature in Christ and of their soul's descent from their Home of Light. Awaken them to thy Call and to the path of personal Christhood that leads to Thee, O Father-Mother of Lights, through the resurrection and the ascension in the Light.

Beloved God Presence, send twelve legions of angels to cut free all souls of Light lost in the shadows who have forgotten the gift of the beautiful Love and Perfection of the Divine Image sealed in their hearts; and bring them to the feet of Christ and the victory over Death and Hell.

Beloved Father-Mother of Lights, I call to you now to enfold all of your children in the seamless garment of the Masterful Christ Presence and to raise them all in *peace, peace, peace* to the beautiful Love and Perfection of the kingdom of Light. Let that kingdom come into manifestation within them through the Light of God that never, never fails to *manifest, manifest, manifest* everywhere I AM!

III

I AM Thy Holy Love!

I AM Thy Secret Love Star!

Alpha and Omega, O Thou the Beginning and the Ending of Cosmos, Thou who in thy beautiful Love and Perfection called forth our twin flames from the fiery ovoid to share in thy Oneness:

Speak thy Divine Will's vibration through our twin flames. Intone it by thy Sacred Word. Transmit it to our Diamond Heart for the re-creation of our worlds in thy Divine Image, our Father-Mother of Lights!

For I AM, we are, thy voice; I AM, we are, thy living temple; I AM, we are, thy heartbeat. Our lives, our souls, our minds, our hearts and our twin flames are one in Thee.

Create, sustain and amplify in our twin flames and in all of thy children a conscious yearning for the coming of thy beautiful Love and Perfection here below, as Above.

Mantrams:

I AM thy Presence
expressing the fiats of eternal Life:

I AM alive forevermore!*

I AM everywhere in the Consciousness of God!*

O Dawn of Everlasting Joy:

I AM my God-victorious ascension in the Light!*

I AM Thy Holy Love!*

I AM Thy Secret Love Star!*

---

*Give this mantram 9 times or in multiples of 27 up to 108.

In the name Jesus Christ
I affirm with my Saviour
in the heart of the Lord
which is, and which was, and which is to come
The Almighty:

**I AM Alpha and Omega,
the Beginning and the Ending!***

O Helios and Vesta, Divine Parents
in the Sun of our solar system, I AM thine!

One in the stream of thy Consciousness
eternally flowing throughout cosmos,
I AM thy Light shining in the Darkness
I AM thy Light-Commanding Presence, commanding:
Light, shine! Light, shine! Light, shine!

I AM thy Power-Wisdom-Love
sustaining every heart and heartbeat
I AM thy Love-Commanding Presence commanding:
Love, rule! Love, rule! Love, rule!

I AM thy Life-Commanding Presence commanding:
O All Life, Ascend!

---

*Give this mantram 9 times or in multiples of 27 up to 108.

IV

Communion Prayer

Our beloved Lord Jesus, as Thou hast said, "Take, eat: this is my body, which is broken for you. . . . This cup is the new testament in my blood: this do in remembrance of me," so come break the Bread of Life with us and pour thy sweet Communion cup. In commemoration of the oneness of the Mystical Body of God in heaven and on earth, we celebrate thy victory over Death and Hell and thy resurrection unto eternal Life.

(All hold thumb and first two fingers of the left hand to the heart and raise the right hand, palm extended toward the bread and the wine, while reading the following paragraphs.)

Centered in the flame of thanksgiving, All One, we share thy Blood and thy Body, the Alpha and the Omega of our Father-Mother God. Come, O Lord, as we are gathered in thy name. Bless now this bread, this wine. Let it carry the full measure of your Christ essence for the renewing of our spiritual natures in this divine alchemy of transubstantiation.

Make us holy, for thou art holy.
Holiness unto the LORD!
Make us worthy, for thou art worthy.
Worthiness unto the LORD!
And let us drink of this fruit of thy Vine new with Thee in the kingdom, even as we partake of it now with beings unascended and beings ascended, Masters, saints, angels and Archangels—glorious beings all one in the Life, Light, Truth and Love of the Divine Mother.

(Conductor raises the altar chalice. All say:)

O Soul of Mine, Ascend!

(Return chalice to its place and partake of Holy Communion.)

By the full Power of the Three-times-Three, in the name of the Father, the Son and the Holy Spirit, it is done.

I AM the Goodness, Peace and Joy of Almighty God manifesting everywhere in the hearts of Christ's communicants worlds without end! Amen.

Prayer to the Father-Mother of Lights

I AM Thy Holy Love!
I AM Thy Secret Love Star!
I AM Alpha and Omega
the Beginning and the Ending!

O Beloved Father-Mother of Lights
In these latter days
speak again to thy children
Let thy voice be heard in us and through us
as we offer ourselves to be living temples
of thy Spirit

I AM Thy Holy Love!
I AM Thy Secret Love Star!
Make our hearts and minds and lives
One in Thee

Grant to all Light-bearers thy peace and freedom
that thy Spirit may prosper in us

Create in us a new heart
Reestablish thy heart tie with our own
Renew in us a right spirit

Cast us not away from thy Presence
but cast away the synthetic self
from our True Self and Thine

Take not thy Holy Spirit from us
but fill us with thy Spirit
Come, O God, enlighten us!

Be with us in the Ending
as Thou wast with us in the Beginning
O Alpha and Omega, our Father-Mother God.
AMEN

Benediction

I AM Thy Holy Love!
I AM Thy Secret Love Star!
watching between each member of the Ashram
as we remain unseparated,
though seemingly apart in time and space,
one in the ocean of thy violet fire,
one in the heart of Freedom's love,
Saint Germain and Portia,
and God-centered in the shining dewdrop
of our own individuality forever:
O Mighty I AM Presence, Thou art One!

PEACE   PEACE   PEACE

OMMMMMMMMMMMMMMMMMMM

General Instructions for Your Altar Set-up:

For your altar you may use a table or dresser covered with an appropriate cloth, preferably white linen. Hang the Chart of Your Divine Self centered above the altar with the Charles Sindelar portraits of Saint Germain and Jesus Christ to the right and left. Place a plain or crystal cup or bowl suitable as a chalice, with a candle on either side, at the center of your altar.

You may choose to have on your altar pictures or statues of Jesus, Mother Mary, Saint Joseph and Archangel Michael as well as of your favorite Ascended Masters or saints, such as Thérèse of Lisieux; one or more vases of fresh or artificial flowers or a flowering plant; a receptacle for burning frankincense; a Bible; and pieces of natural quartz crystal and amethyst crystal. A globe of the world is required, preferably an illuminated globe, to assist in your visualizations. This should be placed on a separate stand.

General Instructions for Conducting Your Rituals:

Conduct your rituals before your altar in a room set aside for your meditations—your sanctum. Burn frankincense to consecrate your sanctum before you begin. When all is in readiness, light two altar candles and stand before your altar in reverence before God, hands cupped to receive the Light rays from on high, even as you open your heart in love to establish the contact with your Father-Mother God. Call to the Ascended Master El Morya, our beloved sponsor, to place his presence in the sanctum throughout your service. During "The Unison Ritual" an instrumental rendition of the "Ave Maria" by Schubert may be played softly as background meditation music while you recite the ritual in the power of the Holy Spirit and your soul's utter devotion.

All the rituals are to be given aloud, whether in group or solitary meditation periods. Throughout the rituals you will find mantrams printed in bold type, which can be memorized and used apart from the rituals. Always give the mantrams 9 times or, optionally, in multiples of 27 up to 108.

At the appropriate place in "The Unison Ritual," you may partake of Holy Communion alone or with your group. Provide individual cups of grape juice and wafers or small pieces of bread. Have them ready on a table at the side of the altar, covered with a white cloth.

2

Great Central Sun Ritual
O Cosmic Christ, Thou Light of the World!
(Sunrise and Sunset)

I

O Cosmic Christ, Thou Light of the World!

In the Beginning Was the Word
And the Word Was with God
And the Word Was God

O Cosmic Christ, Thou Light of the World!
Thou Art Life
And Thy Life Is the Light of My Being

Therefore I AM the True Witness of Thy Light
For Thou Art the True Light
Which Lighteth Every Manifestation
of the Father-Mother God That Cometh into the World

Thou Art the Word Who Was Made Flesh
and Dwelt among Us Full of Grace and Truth
in the Son Jesus Christ

I AM Beholding the Glory of my Lord and Saviour
Jesus Christ
the Glory as of the Only Begotten of the Father
Who Is Also with Me
in My Beloved Holy Christ Self

N.B.: While giving this ritual, turn toward the rising or the setting sun, taking
care not to look directly into it.

II

O Mighty Presence of God, I AM, in and behind the Sun:
I Welcome Thy Light, Which Floods All the Earth
into My Life, into My Mind
into My Spirit, into My Soul.
Radiate and Blaze Forth Thy Light!
Break the Bonds of Darkness and Superstition!
Charge Me with the Great Clearness
of Thy White Fire Radiance!
I AM Thy Child, and Each Day
I Shall Become More of Thy Manifestation!

III

I AM THAT I AM

I AM the Light of the World!*

O Thou Cosmic Christ
Thou the Empowerment of My Sonship through
Jesus Christ
I AM Born Again!
(Not of Blood, nor of the Will of the Flesh
nor of the Will of Man)
but I AM Born of God

For my Lord hath said to me:
"I AM the Resurrection and the Life:
He That Believeth in Me, though He Were Dead,
yet Shall He Live:
and Whosoever Liveth and Believeth in Me
Shall Never Die.
Believest Thou This?"
And I Have Said to Him:
"Yea, Lord: I Believe That Thou Art the Christ,
the Son of God, Which Should Come into the World."

*Give this mantram 9 times or in multiples of 27 up to 108.

Make All Light-bearers of This World and Cosmos One
in the Spirit of the Great White Brotherhood!
We Are One in Thy Mystical Body of the Cosmic Christ.

As Long as I AM in the World
I AM the Light of the World!

Oм   Oм   Oм

IV

Helios and Vesta!
Helios and Vesta!
Helios and Vesta!
Let the Light Flow into My Being!
Let the Light Expand in the Center of My Heart!
Let the Light Expand in the Center of the Earth
And Let the Earth Be Transformed into
the New Day!*

In the Name and in the Footsteps of Jesus Christ:
I AM a Son of God
I AM Come a Light unto the World
That Whosoever Believeth on the Cosmic Christ
Should Not Abide in Darkness
but Should Have the Light of Life

Mantram:
JESUS CHRIST
the Same Yesterday and Today and Forever!*

We Are the Light of the World
Our Ashram, That Is Set on the Hill of the Lord Morya El,
Cannot Be Hid!

*Give this mantram 9 times or in multiples of 27 up to 108.

3

Sacred Ritual for Attunement with God's Holy Will

(Daily at 9:00 a.m. or 9:00 p.m. MST)

I

Our Father, Thy Will Be Done in Us
Teach Us to Love and Accept Thy Will Today
as in Thy Purest Consciousness We Pray
to Be Evermore Like Thee

Heavenly Father-Mother God:
I AM Attuning My Entire Consciousness,
Being and World to Thy Will!
I AM Thy Will Manifesting Today
on Earth as It Is in Heaven!

I AM Born of the Will of God!

Whosoever Shall Do the Will of God
the Same Is My Brother and My Sister and Mother

I AM Led by the Spirit of God!
I AM a Son of God!

O Blessed Holy Spirit
Intercede for Me and the Saints,
That We Should Know What to Pray for;
Intercede for Me and the Saints
According to the Will of God

I AM Affirming and Accepting in the Holy Spirit
That All Things Work Together for Good
to Them That Love God,
to Them Who Are the Called
According to His Purpose
And I AM Grateful!

II

Mantram:

If God Be for Us, Who Can Be Against Us?*

I Present My Body a Living Sacrifice,
Holy, Acceptable unto God,
Which Is My Reasonable Service

I Will Not Be Conformed to This World!
I Will Be Transformed by the Renewing of My Mind,
That I May Prove What Is That Good
and Acceptable and Perfect Will of God

I AM the Servant of Christ
Doing the Will of God from the Heart

I Stand Perfect and Complete in All the Will of God

O My Lord Jesus Christ, I Call for Patience,
That after I Have Done the Will of God
I Might Receive the Promise
of the Coming of My Lord—
My Holy Christ Self

I Shall No Longer Live
the Rest of My Time in the Flesh
to the Lusts of Men
But I Shall Live to the Will of God

*Give this mantram 9 times or in multiples of 27 up to 108.

I Love Not the World
Neither the Things That Are in the World
For the World Passeth Away, and the Lust Thereof:
But He That Doeth the Will of God Abideth Forever

By the Love of God, I Shall Live Forever!

III

Instruction:

Compose your own personal prayer to the LORD God, asking for his Will to be made known to you. Ask for answers to specific questions concerning your plans and projects. Call for the dissolution of all blocks within your psyche to your submission to the Will of God. Ask that all members of the Ashram worldwide and all sons and daughters of the Most High may receive not only attunement with the Holy Will of God but also the deep desire to love and obey it.

Direct your consciousness to the spiritual eye (third eye) at the center of the brow and visualize the white light of the Presence enfolding you completely. See your prayers being answered as the Presence directs powerful, radiant beams of Light through you and all who form the circle of the Ashram—and through them to all servants of the living Christ everywhere.

Keep your attention focused on the beautiful Love and Perfection that God has placed in the Creation as you observe the sacredness of this ritual in deep meditation in the Christ Presence and in attunement with Christ's Love. Make an effort to be alone at the appointed hour or with others who desire to consecrate their lifestreams to the Will of God. If this is not possible, recite the prayers, affirmations and mantrams in mind and heart, silently communing with God and the circle of the Ashram. Fulfill the visualizations and always seal them by Christ-Love directed from your heart.

IV

When you have completed your meditation, visualize a powerful beam of Light going forth from your third eye and your heart chakra to manifest God's Will in specific personal and world situations, as you recite the following mantrams.

Mantrams:

I AM Awake!*

O World, Awake!
Your Dusty Selves Now Shake
Purify and Rectify,
New Ways of Thought to Make!*

Lo! I AM Come to Do Thy Will, O God!*

Not My Will, Not My Will,
Not My Will but Thine Be Done!*

The Will of God Is Good!*

*

*   *

*

Sweet Surrender to Our Holy Vow
(Optional)

Meditation upon the God Flame:

Our will to Thee we sweetly surrender now,
Our will to God Flame we ever bow,
Our will passing into Thine
We sweetly vow.

---

*Give this mantram 9 times or in multiples of 27 up to 108.

Affirmation of the God Flame merging with the heart flame:

No pain in eternal surrender,
Thy Will, O God, be done.
From our hearts the veil now sunder,
Make our wills now one.

Beauty in Thy purpose,
Joy within Thy name,
Life's surrendered purpose
Breathes Thy holy Flame.

Grace within Thee flowing
Into mortal knowing,
On our souls bestowing
Is immortal sowing.

Thy Will be done, O God,
Within us every one.
Thy Will be done, O God—
It is a living sun.

Bestow Thy mantle on us,
Thy garment living flame.
Reveal creative essence,
Come Thou once again.

Thy Will is ever holy,
Thy Will is ever fair.
This *is* my very purpose,
This *is* my living prayer:

Come, come, come, O Will of God,
With dominion souls endow.
Come, come, come, O Will of God,
Restore abundant living now.

Ashram Notes

Today and eternally, we who are called to be the founding stones of the Ashram, as Above so below, are varied personalities woven together as one and merged into the purposes of the Great White Brotherhood through the union of God and the Ascended Masters with our students throughout the world.

The fusion of our lifestreams forms an Ashram of the highest order, providing pilgrims of peace with a bridge between the outer and inner retreats of the adepts and their initiates. Our written communications are Hierarchy's point of contact between Guru and chela.

These will be sent to you, untitled and undated, whenever we deem it necessary, bearing their timeless, nameless quality and the simple heading "Ashram Notes." For easy reference you may choose to keep them in a notebook. We wish to avoid form in the work of the formless, and you will know whereof we speak.

Know that in the establishment of this spiritual edifice, which for God (by permission) I shall humbly call my Ashram, you have been tried and chosen. Know that your real work is soon to begin. We shall labor together for the Lord.

Our principal reason for founding this Ashram is for the linking of hearts worldwide in a ritual of scheduled group meditations. Even though we are separated by time and space, we shall all meet in a union of consciousness, laboring and travailing together to give birth to our Ashram for God.

Sublime is the work entrusted to us by the Infinite One. Sanctified through the chain of Hierarchy, it is comparable to the charge given to the knights of the Holy Grail and the Knights Templar.

You to whom it is given to protect the Brotherhood's work here below must not speak of the Ashram to those not spiritually inclined. We were not given the go-ahead to sponsor this activity until the amanuensis was retaught the importance of silence.

The motto of the Great White Brotherhood, hence of our holy order, is To Know, To Dare, To Do and To Be Silent! The last is perhaps the most important.

No oath is required of you; your soul knows its own divine decree. You are chosen. You are trusted brethren. You also know the sorrows of failure.

Faithfully use the "Great Central Sun Ritual" daily at sunrise or sunset your time. Use the "Ritual for Attunement with God's Holy Will" daily at 9:00 a.m. or 9:00 p.m. and "The Unison Ritual" on the first and third Sundays at 9:30 p.m. MST. And use all three as often as you like.

Keep yourselves pure. You are children of the heavenly hosts.

Eternal blessings,

3

Ashram Notes

As some of you are aware, this scribe has withdrawn into the background for a season. How long this will continue God knows.

The Christ Light will radiate nonetheless from this central Ashram group without interruption; for the Great Creator is above all circumstance. And we must humbly accept our lot, knowing that we have a holy calling from the Most High that must be protected.

These Ashram Notes remain the point of contact with Hierarchy and the ray of their discipline. And for our part, we have offered the little flames of our lives on the altar of God's greatest flame in the service of the Master and those aspiring to be his chelas.

Treason's winds may blow. The laughter of Ishmael against Isaac may assail. We must not partake of gossip. No matter what may be said of us or of anyone in the Ashram, it is well that we have no part with it by writing or talking or even thinking of it.

As Jesus said:

> Let your communication be, Yea, yea;
> Nay, nay: for whatsoever is more than these
> cometh of evil.
>
> Ye have heard that it hath been said, An
> eye for an eye, and a tooth for a tooth: But I say
> unto you, That ye resist not evil: but whosoever
> shall smite thee on thy right cheek, turn to him
> the other also.

How far we would be from outpicturing Christlike lives if we did not apply the catharsis of Love in
every area of our consciousness!

I advocate compassionate forgiveness toward
anyone who has wronged us. Forget the past! Look to
Christ by thinking, speaking and writing of him
under wisdom's guidance—or be silent, still sending
the blessing of courtesy hand to hand, heart to heart.
Always be kind. Let no one upset your peace as you
live your life dedicated to Him.

We who compose this Ashram must apply the
cleansing process of the Christ and his resurrecting
power for our deliverance from past error. Plagued by
the arrows of Darkness that our activities for the Light
have evoked, we as co-workers in the Father's vineyard must take unto ourselves the whole armour of
God, that we may be able to withstand in the evil
day—and in the day of our karma—and, having done
all, to stand.

Even so, through our meditation periods the
Light is raising us to a state of spiritual ecstasy. While
we lay aside our own burden in deference to our service
to Him, let us not forget the burden of humanity. Ours

is to act as channels for Hierarchy and Christ always.

Some think there is naught but bliss in the steps we brothers and sisters occupy. Bliss—yes, but also tension and the burden of the jaded eye upon our efforts.

At times the creative tensions take us to the point of peace. The archives of the Brotherhood record the selfless love of the wayfarers gone before. Yours is the fiat of this moment: to become coordinates for the highest magnets who shall lure men from Satan to God.

My direction may seem slow; yet in centuries past, the Brotherhood's plans and projects have turned to fruition like ripened grain. And now like a whirlwind has this Ashram dimly formed itself. Its manifestation is confined to our lives, our meditations and these contacts.

If we succeed in outpicturing the pattern formed in the heavens, the Most High has promised—as wills surrender to Him and doors are opened to Him—to let the sacred light of Ur of the Chaldees shine again on this plane. And the Ashram of spiritual power shall be known as a temple of the sacred mysteries, if only we shall say in our temples, each one: "Thy will be done!"

Our bodies can knowingly house the Infinite.

For the Infinite One has designed them for his habitation.

Aware of Christ, Adam shall fade through becoming . . .

Eternal blessings,

Mark

4

Ashram Notes

O beloved brethren, shall we say we love not? God knoweth.

But what is best to love—a baked clay vessel whose contents are fire and straw and the fire is not enough to kindle the straw?

Nay, I shall wait a brief moment. The heat cracks the wall a little. The air rushes in, fanning the flame. The straw is consumed. The fire burns on the altar of clay. It fills the whole house till the clay be turned to gold!

This I shall love.

So is everyone that is born of the Spirit.

Maitreya awaits the raising of our Ashramic banner. It is unfurled. *The Mother of the World Is Coming* is written there. For the honor of our sounding is loud and clear: it is for her who loves all, whose compassion the Most High has testified to.

Raise your eyes to the dark skies sprinkled with living flame. Remember, the Christ Mass is eternal; it needs no season. Peace and goodwill need no season. Strengthen their bands. Let your thoughts all be of the Good and the Beautiful.

Gather the stars flaming in God, the moonlight reflecting on the water. *See* the dawn of all that is good and beautiful in the consciousness of men. Gather thou the Son-Light, the soft, white, billowing clouds of His Coming, the winds gently blowing in the flowers while children laugh and play, basking in God's protecting, loving arms.

Realize the meaning of the Harvest. Gather the Good and the Beautiful with God's angels, knowing that they need your transformer-acting consciousness to fill the air with the song of the Lord.

He is riding forth on his white horse. He rides among men today, the redeeming Christ, his vesture dipped in blood—and his name, The Word of God, the King of kings and Lord of lords.

Fill your consciousness with the compassion of the loving, living Christ. See him in the elderly, the tired, the poor, the babes and the struggling parents. See him everywhere in the hearts of the faithful and true.

Gather these thoughts.

Those of you who assembled for our last meeting on the East Coast will remember the discourse on radiation. I give you a new lesson.

First gather the thoughts. Then fix the consciousness simultaneously in the eye of light (the third-eye chakra), in the heart (the heart chakra), and in the place of the sun (the solar plexus).

Then determine by single-eyed vision, and by Christ-wisdom and Christ-love centered in the heart, to use all of your will, multiplied by the will of God (the macrocosmic will) behind your will, in the creative ritual of sowing and reaping.

Your aim is that the good and beautiful thoughts of your harvest may flow forth in waves through the solar-plexus chakra, undulating across the continents and the universes.

For it is written: He that believeth on me, as the scripture hath said, out of his belly (out of the solar-plexus) shall flow rivers of living water.

Finally, determine that these thoughts shall be "permatized" by God to serve the children of the New Age and to assist in preparing the consciousness of the people for the coming of the Divine Mother.

For I say to you, if we *hold our peace*—in "the place of the sun"—the very stones *will* cry out!

Let us all be cleansed, if we will.

Please understand that your devotion is to God. What we say here is a fiat from above to be accepted or not by your willing heart. Accept nothing except it be freely. Give nothing except it be freely. Our directives are subject to your free will. We repeat: Do as you will!

Cleansed of the pseudoself and of the poisons of egoism—jealousy, greed, lust, ambivalence, strife—let us arise as peacemakers between the flesh and the spirit. And let us be one in The Lord Our Righteousness, who is the Peacemaker and Mediator of our souls before the throne of grace.

Break down the middle wall of partition together with the human creation and the human consciousness that created it!

The coming Lord, our Christ, is our peace. The anticipation of the descent of the Lord Christ suddenly into our temple is our peace. We wait upon the Lord. Without him there is no real peace. His peace is a sword that ends all inner strife and the warring in our members.

Peace, peace, peace be unto you.

Eternal blessings,

5

Ashram Notes

O Loving Heart

O loving Heart,
　From whose bounty flows
　Our stream of blessings . . .
Life and Love are thee and thine caressing
　Each tender soul with thine own flame.

O loving Heart,
　Help each one to see
　The Source whence comes our all—
O loving Heart,
　Teach thy wandering child to know
　The meaning of thy care
　Through each moment of thy time—
Till, at one with thee, we shall see
　Thy care for all is ever free.
And burnished with a gleam of fire
　Within thy loving heart,
　May our cup like thine forever be:
　O loving Heart!

N.B. This poem may be recited as a prayer with your "Ritual for Soul Purification."

When spring is in the process of formation, it is well to let the consciousness dwell on the Good and the Beautiful. Think of how the Mother of the World spreads a green carpet over all, the healing green meeting the diamond-blue sky, all basking in the pure wisdom-gold of the sun.

Transformation should be the goal of the Christ consciousness individually manifest. Dwell not on little things of finite self. Every one of you, as you read this, must realize that in your Real Self *you are a mahatma,* and as such I salute you.

Yes, we speak of goal-fittedness. We send forth the Call. Likewise call to us when in need:

Brethren, pray for me lest I fall.

O let me learn to love my God with my whole heart! I cannot deny thee, O Beloved, thou who hast blessed me so richly with the Holy Presence of thyself. O my God, my Guru, come into my temple this day!

The Ashram is a true watchtower, invisible yet mighty. Let light and compassion flow to the world; may many be redeemed.

"Run, not as uncertainly; fight, not as one that beateth the air," was the thought of a great saint. "Strive for mastery; keep body and soul under subjection to the Great Lawgiver; be not a castaway" was his self-reminder.

From Gethsemanes and crucifixions comes the glory of the resurrection and the ascension. Remember the parable of the wise and foolish virgins and the oil that was needed for their lamps. May we have oil in our lamps. For the Bridegroom cometh.

The periods of meditation are bearing fruit. A more Christlike character emerges in the participants, displacing the weaknesses of the outer personality. Becoming more Christlike as we fulfill the ritual of our meditations means standing in and for the Ashramic consciousness.

We shall embody a fuller Light than they of earth dream of.

We must make ourselves ready to stand in this Light. It is not of earth, yet earth shall rise because of it and we shall endure. The heat of the Flame without the Light would consume. It is the Light that cools and transmutes. The Flame makes malleable, the Light changes!

Exercise the mantrams we give you herewith to achieve catharsis in preparation for a higher union with the holy rays. *See* the action of your words taking place before your eyes. Practice harmonization of the outer self with the Inner Self.

Make ready the soul for fusion with God.

Produce within your seven chakras the white light from the LORD's rainbow. Fill all your house with this white light. This is the preparatory ray whereby you shall be tested in the Masters' service and your lifestreams eventually used in the redemption of humanity.

Prepare for battle yet serve the divine warriors. Hail, Arjuna! Hail, O Lord Krishna, our Divine Guide!

Give the enclosed "Ritual for Soul Purification" before retiring or whenever guided from God.

*   *   *

From an ashram for God there comes a message from a beloved Brother who has long held a high spiritual office. I bow to the hierophant and friend of Christ, Koot Hoomi Lal Singh.

Salutations in Light!

The ashramic harmonies bear relation to the laws of music. For the laws of harmony applied by musicians are but reflections of the higher melodic laws; and the tonal perfection of the infinite harmonies emanating from the Light is the outpicturing in sound of the Law that holds together the atoms of creation.

Love is the master pitch pipe of all life. My hope is that your worldwide Ashram shall harmonize with Love. Then you will be safe. For you will tread the infinite wheel of light, color and sound in the inner consciousness of the One, and of the ones who have become Brothers on every plane.

Your Ashram will be for God as you give yourself to him. Walk in the Light toward the ray and the sound of the OM.

KH

It is known that all in our circle of meditation are being blessed. It is realized that spiritual and worldly duties at times hinder participation in our rituals. At some contact points all are present, at others not. Whenever possible strive to be in tune and to stay in tune, even while fulfilling obligations.

May the rays of Divine Love permeate every pore of your being, radiating new life out into the community, spreading the message of spring everywhere.

Eternal blessings,

M.

4

Sacred Ritual for Soul Purification
(Before Retiring)

I

Infinite Light!

Infinite Light!
  Shine now in the cave of being,
  Fill me completely with Light!

Infinite Light!
  Let shadows stand out, loom largely,
  And fade quickly at the blasts of Light from Thee!

Infinite Light!
  I AM one with God and Light,
  All Darkness flees before thy holy Light!

Infinite Light!
  Flee, lust! Flee, greed! Flee, jealousy! Flee, hatred!
  Flee, selfishness! Flee, laziness! Flee, unkindness!
  Flee, *all* hurts! Flee, *all* wounds!

  Flee, every thought that is less than Light!
  Flee, every feeling that is less than Light!
  Flee, every motive that is less than Light!
  Flee, every word and deed that is less than Light!

II

C o m e !

O Christlike purity, Come!
Flow into me and from me.
Love, selflessness,
Godly ambition and kindness to all,

Come!

I Will Be Christlike!

In the name of the Father
    I will be Christlike!
In the name of the Son
    I will be Christlike!
In the name of the Holy Spirit
    I will be Christlike!
In the name of the Mother of the World
    I will be Christlike!

Fill me, O Christ, Thou Light of the world!
Fill me, O Christ, Thou Light of the world!
Fill me, O Christ, Thou Light of the world!

III

My soul doth magnify the Lord!*

And my spirit hath rejoiced in God my Saviour!*

---

*Give this mantram 9 times or in multiples of 27 up to 108.

IV
(Optional Section)

Prayer for My Soul's Awakening

Look through my soul, O Christ divine
    Now let thy fire my world refine
Look through my heart, O "I AM" of me
    From wrong desires now set me free.

Refrain:
    Lovingly now I wait for Thee
    Gladly, O God, thy will to see
    Lift me to Thee, illumine me
    Spirit divine.

Look through my eyes, O Light of Truth
    Teach me thy law, eternal youth
Place in my hands thy wonderful key
    That shall unlock the door for me.

Speak and my ears shall hear thy voice
    Angelic choirs with me rejoice
Guide now my feet, no more let me roam
    From that one Path that leads all Home.

N.B. You may recite this prayer or sing it to the hymn melody for "Open my eyes that I may see" by Charles H. Scott.

The Twenty-Third Psalm
A Psalm of David

The LORD is my Shepherd:
I shall not want.
He maketh me to lie down in green pastures: he leadeth me beside the still waters.
He restoreth my soul: he leadeth me in the paths of righteousness for his name's sake.
Yea, though I walk through the valley of the shadow of death, I will fear no evil: for thou art with me; thy rod and thy staff they comfort me.
Thou preparest a table before me in the presence of mine enemies: thou anointest my head with oil; my cup runneth over.
Surely goodness and mercy shall follow me all the days of my life: and I will dwell in the house of the LORD for ever.

Ashram Notes

The auspicious hour for the giving of the enclosed "Sacred Ritual for Transport and Holy Work" is just before you retire, when the bridge to the infinite is being lowered, the mundane events of the day are dimmed, and the soul prepares herself to unite with God's omnipresence.

This ritual is intended to assist you in performing a holy and a mighty work for humanity during the hours of repose, after you temporarily fold the body-tent so that you may more consciously reside in the house of the Infinite One.

May these hours of bodily rest be hours of freedom for your soul's activity in the octaves of Light, when she is free from the prison house of physical and mental form and the confines of the ego; and withal may you help struggling kindred souls in their efforts to escape the cyclic, rebounding effects of negative karma.

As you travel out of the body, may your shield be the I AM THAT I AM, the Omnipotent One, who is continually radiating the Divine Will that is the heartbeat of the universe.

Under the protection of Archangel Michael and his legions, may you perform the Divine Will everywhere on this planet and do what your lesser ego in body-prison could never do: assist in bringing the message of the Universal Christ consciousness to souls from all walks of life — "all nations and kindreds and people and tongues." And through your loving ministrations every eye *shall* behold him.

It is within our field of endeavor in this Ashram to minister as Christed* ones to the souls of earth. For even Christ during the three days of his entombment did preach without the body† to souls not yet liberated from the astral prison forged by their Atlantean karma.

You, too, during these days of your entombment in matter, may freely arise in Christ consciousness; you may put on the white robes of your righteousness and thus use your God-given etheric body as a vehicle to express the vibrations of the coming age and race before their time.

Your work is the work of pioneers, yet there are those who have gone before! The trailblazers who lighted the universe — Christ and Krishna — remain to succor you and show you the way.

Through our efforts may many journey in humility to the manger of their hearts and kneel before the Manchild born of the Divine Mother. May they grow with him to adolescence to discourse with and lay bare worldly doctors in temples of religion, and to mature to their divinity through temptations and afflictions.

And may they come to the place where their "greatest of earth born of woman," the John the Baptist

---

*The word *Christ* is derived from the Greek *Christos*, meaning "anointed"; thus the Christed ones are the "anointed ones."

†out of the body. Apart from his physical body the spirit of our Lord did descend to the astral plane; as it is stated in the Apostle's Creed, "He descended into hell."

of their own physical and mental selfhood, does defer to the Son of God and does baptize and anoint that Christ who is come to manhood in themselves.

Knees bowed, may the tutored self proclaim itself not worthy to loose the shoelaces of the Christed soul but instead acclaim the Christ now risen to the sanctum sanctorum. And may the human ego bow to the Lord of lords, and the Divine Ego triumph over matter.

In due time may the many begin their individual missions of proclaiming the Infinite One as Lord of Life. May they be willing to be crucified on the cross of the desire body, to not only die daily with him but also to live daily in his consciousness until the power of his resurrection surges through the root and the stalk and the flower of the self.

Then will they stand supreme, one by one, alone on the battlefield, victorious over all, conqueror of the self, one with the God Self. Being absorbed by this Higher Consciousness and then scattered from the mountaintop as in a cloud of glory, they will come in like manner by decree of the I AM THAT I AM—the Paramatman,* or Supreme Atman—one forever, while aeons cycle, with absolute peace reigning over all.

We are committed to this Ashram's high and holy purpose: the spreading of the message of the Inner Christ, the awakening and the strengthening of all Brotherhoods of Light and all true initiates thereof, the dispersal of Darkness by Light, and the relieving of sorrow by joy.

---

*Paramatman [Sanskrit, param, "supreme"; atman, "Spirit," or "Self," i.e., the inner essence of the universe or of man that is one with Brahman]: in Hinduism, the supreme Self or Spirit; God; Brahman.

And we shall carry on the noblest traditions of the Great White Brotherhood, secure in the knowledge that our God will not be mocked—as we sow so shall we reap! And God, who is faithful, will help us who faithfully work for him.

With this noble dedication may we go forth confident in the Lord, who will raise us up as his servants in this holy work. To those who bore the message long ago, Paul said:

> For ye see your calling, brethren, how that not many wise men after the flesh, not many mighty, not many noble, are called:

> But God hath chosen the foolish things of the world to confound the wise; and God hath chosen the weak things of the world to confound the things which are mighty;

> And base things of the world, and things which are despised, hath God chosen, yea, and things which are not, to bring to nought things that are:

> That no flesh should glory in his presence.

> But of him are ye in Christ Jesus, who of God is made unto us wisdom, and righteousness, and sanctification, and redemption:

> That, according as it is written, He that glorieth, let him glory in the Lord.

Let us *know* that before us, leading in the dissemination of profound Love, is the Christ—the Lux Regius—our Holy Brother Jesus, whose Galilean ministry laid the foundation of his work that we must build on today.

His legions in the fore, his mantram ringing clear—"Lo! the I AM THAT I AM of me is with you alway, even to the end of the Piscean age"—he calls our souls and we answer, enlisted in the service of the King.

With deepest blessing I entrust this "Sacred Ritual for Transport and Holy Work" to your keeping.

Eternally,

5

Sacred Ritual for Transport and Holy Work
(Before Retiring)

I

Mantrams for the Stilling of the Four Lower Bodies

"Blessed are the peacemakers:
for they shall be called the children of God"

"Peace I leave with you
My Peace I give unto you"
                        Jesus

Angels of Peace
Elohim of Peace
Seal my four lower bodies
Remove all barriers
impeding my soul's full and radiant reflection
of my Mighty I AM Presence and Holy Christ Self
to the glory of God

In the Peace-Commanding Presence
of the Cosmic Christ!
In the name Jesus Christ
I command my four lower bodies:

Mantrams:
Peace Be Still!*
Be Still and Know That I AM God*—
I Will Be Exalted in the Heavens!
I Will Be Exalted in the Earth!

The LORD God of Hosts is with us
He is our refuge and strength
A very present help in trouble

Thou Ancient of Days, my Lord Sanat Kumara, Great Guru of Light, Life, Love and Holy Wisdom, Thou who art our sponsor for the rescue of all children of the Light and Light-bearers, worlds without end: I bow before the God Flame within thee in gratitude for thy Presence in the universe and I thank thee and thy legions of angels who protect and defend us in Armageddon.

Be with me this night as I go forth to do thy assigned Holy Work. Transport my soul safely from my abode to my destination(s) and back again. In the service of the King of kings and Lord of lords, I remain faithful to my vows to thee in the Beginning and the Ending of my sojourn in this Matter universe. Amen.

II

Prayer for Forgiveness

Mindful of the admonition "Let not the sun go down upon your wrath," I would set my house in order before I begin my "Sacred Ritual for Transport and Holy Work."

O Christ and Krishna, with joy I forgive all who have harmed me. With joy I forgive all who should ever cast a shadow to harm me past, present or future.

*Give this mantram 9 times or in multiples of 27 up to 108.

In the I AM THAT I AM, I rise above all harm and I affirm that Christ in me is the Harmless One and I declare that Divine Love is supreme and to be desired above all desiring.

Multiply in my soul undying love for God, Life, Light, Truth and Love, and for the Creation by Elohim. Teach me to make right the wrong, to undo the miscreations I have created in ignorance of or in willful disobedience to thy Great Law. Withdraw thy sacred energies from my miscreations by the Great Central Sun Magnet. Demagnetize and transmute these energies and reconsecrate them to thy perfect creations, which I ask to be brought forth through me and all Light-bearers.

Remembering the words of Our Lord "If ye forgive men their trespasses, your heavenly Father will also forgive you: But if ye forgive not men their trespasses, neither will your Father forgive your trespasses," I pray:

In the name of the Father, the Son and the Holy Spirit, I invoke forgiveness for myself for all wrongs I have ever committed against Life; and I forgive all who have ever committed wrongs against me—and I call upon the law of forgiveness in their behalf.

Mantram:

> I AM Forgiveness acting here,
> Casting out all doubt and fear,
> Setting men forever free
> With wings of cosmic Victory.
>
> I AM calling in full power
> For Forgiveness every hour;
> To all life in every place
> I flood forth forgiving Grace.*

---

*Give this mantram 3 times, 9 times or in multiples of 27 up to 108.

Mantrams for Intercession
to Kuan Yin, the Goddess of Mercy

NA-MO   KUAN   SHIH   YIN   P'U-SA*
NAH-MO GWAN SHE(R)† EEN POO-SAH

Hail! (Homage to the sacred name of)
Bodhisattva Kuan Shih Yin

CHIU   K'U   CHIU   NAN   P'U-SA   LAI*
JEE OH KOO JEE OH NAHN POO-SAH LYE

Save from suffering, save from calamity,
Bodhisattva—come!

III

Pledge to Christ and Krishna

In the name I AM THAT I AM, I bow before
the polestar of my Being, the Great God Presence. As
a member of El Morya's Ashram, I declare my Father-
Mother God to be my eternal goal and the Great
Central Sun to be my Home.

Through Christ and Krishna I chart my course
by free will through these matter spheres, in wisdom
and loving obedience to thy laws. By thy grace I AM
fulfilling the path of righteousness that leads to Thee.
For by thy grace I AM a Christed one.

And this is my divine decree, uttered unalterably
in the name of the Son of God Jesus Christ and the
Lord Krishna. I speak it this day and I renew it each
day through my soul-guided determination to serve my
God of Life, Light, Truth and Love. So be it.

---

*Give this mantram 3 times, 9 times or in multiples of 27 up to 108.
†(R) indicates the pronunciation of a light r.

I pledge myself and I offer my soul-faculties and vehicles and all that I am and ever shall be to Christ and Krishna. I pledge to minister to all Light-bearers of the world as God and Hierarchy shall direct, that they may shed the cocoon of ignorance and awaken to their Mighty I AM Presence and Holy Christ Self and to our joint ministry in the Light. Take me, use me, assimilate me, O God of Life, Light, Truth and Love.

I pledge undying enmity with the five poisons and I call to the Five Dhyani Buddhas for that specific gift of Wisdom that is the antidote to these poisons.

On behalf of all
Sons of God, I call:

OM VAIROCHANA OM!
Flood us with
the All-Pervading Wisdom of the Dharmakaya,
my Mighty I AM Presence.
By thy sacred fire consume in me
the poison of ignorance!

OM AKSHOBHYA HUM!
Flood us with Mirrorlike Wisdom.
By thy sacred fire consume in me
the poison of all
anger and hate and hate creation!

OM RATNASAMBHAVA TRAM!
Flood us with the Wisdom of Equality.
By thy sacred fire consume in me
the poison of
spiritual, intellectual and human pride!

OM AMITABHA HRIH!
Flood us with Discriminating Wisdom.
By thy sacred fire consume in me
the poisons of the passions—
all cravings, covetousness, greed and lust!

OM AMOGHASIDDHI AH!
Flood us with All-Accomplishing Wisdom,
the Wisdom of Perfected Action.
By thy sacred fire consume in me
the poisons of envy and jealousy.

OM VAJRASATTVA HUM!
Flood us with the Wisdom
of the Diamond Will of God.
By thy sacred fire consume in me
the poisons of non-Will and non-Being:
fear, doubt and non-belief in God, the Great Guru.

COME VAIROCHANA! COME AKSHOBHYA!
COME RATNASAMBHAVA!
COME AMITABHA! COME AMOGHASIDDHI!
COME VAJRASATTVA!

OM HUM TRAM HRIH AH HUM

OMMMMMMMMMMMMMMMMMM

Father, may the divine vibrations of thy Word
be channeled to the physical octaves through my
voice upraised in prayer and adoration to thy Name
I AM THAT I AM—OM. May thy Word fulfill thy
divine decree in me, and may my soul go forth this
night to fulfill what my free will in obedience to thy
Will, thy Love and thy Wisdom has decreed and what
my voice and heart have spoken.   Amen.

IV

Prayer and Visualization
for Transport and Holy Work

Father, into thy hands I commend my spirit.
O my soul, let us arise from our abode.
Mighty I AM Presence and Holy Christ Self,
with Archangel Michael and a cordon of blue lightning angels, transport my soul clothed in my finer
bodies, fully equipped with the armour of God, to the
designated place of my Holy Work this night. Escort
me, instruct me, and guide and protect me and all
co-servers, I pray Thee, now and always as we serve
to cut free all life on earth.

The LORD Is My Keeper

I will lift up mine eyes unto the hills,
from whence cometh my help.
My help cometh from the LORD,
the I AM THAT I AM,
which made heaven and earth.
He will not suffer my foot to be moved:
he that keepeth me will not slumber.
Behold, he that keepeth Israel
shall neither slumber nor sleep.
The LORD is my Keeper:
the LORD, my Mighty I AM Presence,
is my shade upon my right hand.
The sun shall not smite me by day,
nor the moon by night.

The LORD shall preserve me from all evil:
he shall preserve my soul.
The LORD shall preserve my going out
and my coming in from this time forth,
and even for evermore.

Mantrams:

Lord Michael before!
Lord Michael behind!
Lord Michael to the right!
Lord Michael to the left!
Lord Michael above!
Lord Michael below!
Lord Michael, Lord Michael wherever I go!
I AM his Love protecting here!
I AM his Love protecting here!
I AM his Love protecting here!*

In the Name Archangel Michael:
Evil Is Not Real and Its Appearance Has No Power!*

Instruction:

If you know where you are going for your Holy Work, first point to the location on the globe where you are and then to the location where you are going. Trace a direct route with your index finger from your home base, or wherever you happen to be, to the obelisk of the Washington Monument in Washington, D.C. (38°54′N, 77°01′W). At the monument, a focus of the Ascended Masters, you will meet brother and sister Ashram workers. From this point of useful focalization, our spiritual directors, the Ascended Masters, will guide your group to the assigned destination of the night's Holy Work that is before you. If you know your destination in advance, trace a direct route on the globe from the Washington Monument to that destination.

*Give this mantram 3 times, 9 times or in multiples of 27 up to 108.

During times of the generation of world tension, use this exercise to transport your soul to the area of tension, no matter where on earth, and minister to those in need. Always trace your route on the globe, heading straight for the Washington Monument first. It will help fix in consciousness the goal. Then proceed with the co-servers who have gathered there to the coordinated assignment.

If you are not certain of your ultimate destination, you can be certain you will be directed from inner levels. It is essential to always make the call:

Beloved God Presence, Lord Christ and Lord Krishna with the ascended Brethren, enfold me in an aura of your Cosmic Christ radiance and accompany me to the place prepared where I may serve my God and my people in thy Holy Work assigned to me this night according to the will of God, to_____
_____(name the place if you know it)_____ or wherever I am needed by the Hierarchy to perform their Holy Work.

In the name of the God of all Life, Light, Truth and Love and for the purposes of the Father-Mother God and the Brotherhood of all servants of the Light, I arise from Matter's maya and density and from my physical form into the Holy Spirit.

I AM here! And I AM come to do thy will, O Lord Christ, O Lord Krishna, on earth as it is decreed in heaven!

Instruction:

Visualize the Light of the Universal Christ and the Universal Krishna surrounding you and all Light-bearers engaged in the Holy Work while intoning these sounds of the Word:

In the power of my God, I chant:

THUURRRRRRRRRRRRRRRRRRRRRR (deep)

OMMMMMMMMMMMMMMMMMMMMMMMM

OHHHHHHHHHHHHHHHHHHHHHHHHHHHHH

ELLLLLLLLLLLLLLLLLLLLLLLLLLLLL

URRRRRRRRRRRRRRRRRRRRRRRRRRRR (very deep)

Instruction:

In conclusion press your hands together over your heart. Allow yourself to feel your deepest devotion to the LORD God in the Great Central Sun, to his individualized I AM Presence and Holy Christ Self and God Flame with you. And let your devotion be also to the Light in all saints and ascended and unascended Masters, as Above, so below. With reverence and humility lift your consciousness skyward.

Before entering sleep visualize the obelisk of the Washington Monument in a shaft of white light and fix the goal in your mind's eye. A postcard or large framed photograph of the monument, kept in your bedroom, will help your soul make physical contact with the spot. This exercise should be rehearsed as you fall asleep, for thereby you direct your consciousness to the destined rendezvous of co-servers in the Light.

Looking out over the reflecting pool, which extends from the monument to the Lincoln Memorial, contemplate the mystery of the soul as a mirror of the Spirit of the living God. See the soul herself as the reflecting pool but also look into the pool to see the image of your face becoming the Divine Image, in whose likeness you were made. Then see your soul and the souls of the co-servers merging with the Holy Spirit of the I AM Presence above you. See your soul rise from the reflecting pool as the Presence draws nigh and say the mantram aloud as you meditate on the God Flame in your heart:

O God! I claim the promise:
I AM drawing nigh to Thee.
Draw Thou nigh to me!*

One with the Presence, I affirm:
I AM merging my entire
consciousness, being and world
with the Spirit of my Lord Christ
and my Lord Krishna,
according to the divine plan
of my soul's journey this night.*

O Christ!

I AM THAT I AM
I AM the Open Door which no man can shut
I AM the Light which lighteth every man
    that cometh into the world
I AM the Way
I AM the Truth
I AM the Life
I AM the Resurrection
I AM the Ascension in the Light
I AM the fulfillment of all my needs
    and requirements of the hour
I AM abundant Supply poured out upon all Life
I AM perfect Sight and Hearing
I AM the manifest Perfection of being
I AM the illimitable Light of God
    made manifest everywhere
I AM the Light of the Holy of Holies
I AM a son of God
I AM the Light in the holy mountain of God

*Give this mantram 9 times or in multiples of 27 up to 108.

O Krishna!

**Hare Krishna, Hare Krishna
Krishna Krishna, Hare hare
Hare Rama, Hare Rama
Rama Rama, Hare hare***

Behold, what manner of love
the Father hath bestowed upon us
that we should be called the Sons of God:
therefore the world knoweth us not,
because it knew him not.
Beloved, now are we the Sons of God,
and it doth not yet appear what we shall be:
but we know that, when he shall appear,
we shall be like him;
for we shall see him as he is.
And every man that hath this hope in him
purifieth himself,
even as he is pure.

I John 3:1–3

The Earth is the LORD'S and the fulness thereof!*
the world and they that dwell therein.

Instruction:
You can repeat this visualization and meditation on
the soul merging with the Spirit at other great world
shrines situated near a body of water, such as:
The Grand Teton mountain near Jackson, northwest-
ern Wyoming, the United States of America (43°50′N,

*Give this mantram 9 times or in multiples of 27 up to 108.

110°55′W), elevation 13,770 feet. The Grand Teton is the tallest of three massive peaks called the Cathedral Group, which rise 7,000 feet above the Jackson Hole valley. These are reflected in a number of surrounding lakes but most spectacularly in nearby Jenny Lake, the second-biggest lake in Grand Teton National Park.

Congruent with the mountain on the etheric plane is the Royal Teton Retreat, preeminent retreat of the Great White Brotherhood on the North American continent, where all souls who are willing to diligently pursue the path of self-mastery are invited to study in their finer bodies under the Ascended Master Saint Germain. It was at this spot that the Archangels first descended to earth and the first root races (groups of souls) took embodiment.

Victoria Mountain (51°26′N, 116°11′W), near Banff, Alberta, Canada, reflected in Lake Louise (1.5 miles long). Along with many of the lakes in the area, Lake Louise is colored a unique aquamarine because of chalk-like mineral deposits in the glacial runoff. At the etheric retreat of Archangel Michael within the mountain, countless legions of blue-lightning angels come and go on their missions to rescue the Light-bearers of the world.

The Taj Mahal near Agra, Uttar Pradesh state, northern India (27°12′N, 77°59′E). Beginning in 1632 Shah Jahan, the fifth Mogul Emperor of India (an incarnation of the Master Kuthumi), built the Taj Mahal as a monument to his wife and constant companion, Mumtaz Mahal, who had died in childbirth. The structure took twenty-two years to complete.

The sacred places at Varanasi (also known as Benares) on the Ganges, Varanasi district, Uttar Pradesh state, northern India (25°20′N, 83°00′E). The city sits in a four-mile sweep along the Ganges River. Hindus go to Varanasi to die since by so doing they are reputedly guaranteed entrance into Shiva's heaven and freedom from the round of rebirth. There are fifteen hundred temples of different sects in Varanasi, many of which line the river. Leading down to the water from the temples are wide flights of steps, or *ghats*, used by the thousands of Hindus who bathe in the sacred water each morning, saying their prayers as they face the rising sun.

The temple of Brahma on the holy Lake Pushkar, Ajmer district, Rajasthan state, India (26°30'N, 74°33'E). According to legend, the lake was formed from water that sprang forth from three places touched by a lotus blossom that Brahma let fall from heaven. Another story says that Brahma bathed in the lake as a penance. This is one of the few temples in all of India that is devoted to Brahma exclusively.

The ruins of a temple to the Sun on the Island of the Sun in Lake Titicaca, western Bolivia (16°01'S, 69°10'W). By legend, the ruins mark the spot where the two founders of the Inca dynasty were sent down to the earth by the Sun. The lake is 3,205 square miles and, at 12,500 feet, is the world's highest navigable lake.

The most sacred of all of these places and the fulcrum of the East—Mount Kailas in southwest Tibet, (31°00'N, 82°00'E), the holiest of all Himalayan peaks. It, together with Lake Manasarowar at its southern foot, is the goal of Hindu and Buddhist pilgrims and can be yours as a part of your nightly Holy Work. Hindus believe it is the location of the paradise of Shiva. Sanskrit texts compare it to the metaphysical Mount Meru, or Sumeru, the cosmic center of the universe.

Kailas is 22,028 feet high and Lake Manasarowar, at 14,950 feet, is said to be the world's highest freshwater lake. According to Lama Govinda, it is "shaped like the sun and represents the forces of light. . . . 'Manas' (Sanskrit) means mind or consciousness: the seat of the forces of cognition, of light, and finally of enlightenment."

Ashram Notes

Brethren,

As the season of the Christ Mass draws near, let us do our best in using our wills, harnessed to God's will, for the upliftment of those who are in bondage to maya and the forces of Darkness.

Consider the force of a magnet. When the steel comes close to the magnet, the magnet draws it quickly to itself; but when the steel is farther away, the magnet's pull can be measured only with the most sensitive instruments.

Remember the magnet of Love. The heart magnetizes the soul and measures the soul's response. But how shall the unawakened soul respond to the pull of the heart?

It is meet that we bear the tensions of men. Bearing one another's burdens, we fulfill the law of Christ. For the Great Guru, like Atlas of old, has ever carried the burden of the world. Let us be helpers of the Christ, sharing the cross of Love.

Remember, the Master fell under the karmic load. Shall not the crown of thorns pierce our own heads?

Attached is the "Sacred Ritual for Oneness" delivered to my amanuensis this night in his sanctum. Its efficacy is tested. It lies in the hidden responses of the soul.

I invite all of you to join me on Christmas Eve at eleven o'clock (or at the hour of your choice) as we pass the torch of the Christ Mass from time belt to time belt around the world in a high and holy meditation period.

We shall begin with "The Unison Ritual." Then we shall give the "Sacred Ritual for Oneness" followed by the "Sacred Ritual for Transport and Holy Work." (We will omit the world globe tracing, which each one may elect to complete at home before retiring.)

Thus journey to Shamballa by the arrow of thought. Upon retiring let the soul follow the arrow to accomplish for humanity that which can only be done in the etheric body beyond the veil.

May the world be better for our striving to bring the forces of Light to the fore. Remember, you are not alone. God and the great Masters are ever with you as you work together to enlighten the few and to ease the terrible sorrow borne by the many.

At this season pray for the healing of world crisis; be mindful to call for the illumination of presidents, kings and rulers of all lands as well as of all citizens of the world and their elected representatives.

As Aquarius dawns let us give birth to a fuller measure of cooperation and love, that the song "Glory to God in the highest, and on earth peace, goodwill toward men" might become a reality in the souls of all people. Though the phrases be worn by the tongues of men, until their souls realize the true meaning the earth shall not be free.

May the peace of God abide in all hearts this Christmas Eve, even as it is carried everywhere on earth by the angels of Christ's birth.

With deepest blessings and peace
I keep the vigil at his manger in your hearts,

6

Sacred Ritual for Oneness
(First and Third Sundays)

Instruction:
   This ritual follows "The Unison Ritual" on the first and third Sundays. You may also give it prior to the "Sacred Ritual for Transport and Holy Work" before retiring. It is the grand gateway to your participation with Hierarchy. In addition, use it when the direction is given from the central Ashram group or whenever you are moved by the Holy Spirit. The devout and those who lead a monastic life may choose to use it daily. Like all of our rituals, it is to be given aloud whether in group or solitary meditation periods.

I

I Would Remain...

   I would gladly give my all if with Lord Krishna I might permeate the universe with one fragment of myself—and remain...
   I would remain on earth a pilgrim of peace.
   I would remain in heaven in the peace of the Divine Whole.
   I would remain as a comforter to all:
   A Good Samaritan to the wounded and the suffering,
      A friend to the friendless,
      The voice of conscience to the conscienceless,
      Father to the fatherless,
      Mother to the motherless,

Brother or sister to the orphan, giving even my body and my blood to those who hunger and thirst after righteousness.

I would heal the sick, cleanse the lepers, raise the dead, and cast out devils in Christ's name; for freely I have received and freely I shall give.

I would be an eternal Light like God, to dispel the Darkness of world suffering.

For all whom Christ would deliver through me, I would even be one with Pain and Death to break the cursed bonds asunder.

That the lightening of thy coming, O Lord, and thy resurrection power may penetrate space is my prayer and my meditation this hour.

Hallowed be thy name I AM THAT I AM, Thou who doest hallow and make One the souls who are the many.

I Climb the Ladder!

All links dissolve in the Presence
Divine Holy Will, come into me
One alone is the All-One
I AM THAT I AM is that One
I decree it and it is done

Light!   Light!   Light!

Instruction:

    Concentrate on the point of the third-eye chakra at the brow. Establish contact with God by holding in your "mind's eye" the highest Divine Image of God you can conceive of. Then visualize a powerful ray of Light going forth from your Mighty I AM Presence through your third eye as a bright beacon, lighting the way Home for the children of God. Repeat this mantram 9 times or in multiples of 27 up to 108:

In the name of Almighty God, I will my Light to shine!

Feel both the personal and impersonal love of your Holy Christ Self radiating to all children of the Light from the point of your heart chakra. As you intensify God's love for you and your love for him in your heart, visualize your heart chakra as a focus of the golden pink glow-ray from the heart of Helios and Vesta. Your heart overflowing with Gratitude, Love and Light, give this mantram 9 times or in multiples of 27 up to 108:

O God, my heart chalice runneth over!

As you intone the sound of the Ur[1] to release the Light of your heart, visualize a powerful beam of Light emanating from your heart chakra. This is the ray of God, the Great Guru—the Dispeller of Darkness—passing through the chela.

U R R R R R R R R R R R R R R R R R R

By the Divine Will
my Love and Light all thine
covers thy omnipresence all mine
I AM focalizing the white light on this planet,
leading colors, vibrations, virtues,
rays and races to their divine oneness in Spirit

O Jesus!
O Hermes Trismegistus![2]
O Maitreya!

(Intone the 5 vowel sounds 3 times in this order: I O E U A)

IIIIII-OOOOOH-EEEEEE-OOOOOO-AAAAAH

II
Divine Mother
in thy power and name
and the presence of thy Sons, call I:

Lead me to Shamballa
City of Light—City of the Sun—City of the Soul

* *
*

My single eye of Light is suddenly aflame with Christ
The blue beauty of the star of the East draws nigh
within the Eden of my sacred self!

Smiling upon me, kindred souls of the Brotherhood
of that Holy City greet me with a holy kiss
I am enraptured with bliss and
I will share my holy joy forever in thy name
my Saviour Jesus Christ

To thee I send

Roses   Roses   Roses

O my soul!
Thou art becoming one with God

Out of my oneness with the All-in-all
I pledge undying love
Clasping hands with the Brethren and my Christ
I AM coming home to Shamballa, City of Light

I AM sealed in the OM
on the sacred altar of Love

III

In the pure white Flame of the pure white Light
I AM emanating Love from the sacred centers of my being

By the rainbow spheres of God
I AM holding the children of the Light in
pure blue, pure rose, pure yellow,
pure green, pure purple, pure violet
of the Great Blue Causal Body

I AM become the One
the One I AM become

In my mind forever oneness with Morya El
In my heart forever   oneness with Morya El
In my soul forever   oneness with Morya El

By the midnight blue of the Divine Mother
and her great starry blue canopy of Light
I AM establishing forever and forever
my oneness with the Master Morya El
holding him
in my mind forever
holding him
in my heart forever
holding him
in my soul forever

Pluribus Unum - Unum Pluribus

RA MA   RA MA   RA MA

OM   OM   OM   OM   OM   OM   OM

IV

I abide this night in Shamballa
City of my God.
Pilgrim of peace from Terra, I pray, O LORD
for the Oneness of my soul in thy Spirit tonight.
As I dwell in the City of the Eternal Day
tears of joy mingle with the tears of the saints
in Love's resolution.

And God shall wipe away all tears from our eyes
and there shall be no more death, neither sorrow
nor crying, neither shall there be any more pain
for the former things are passed away.

And he that sat upon the throne said
Behold, I make all things new.

Into this starry city

through the gateway of the holy star

I see my God before me:

I AM come

merging my all with the One

*

O Star of my God Presence

I AM THAT I AM

OMMMMMMMMMMMMMMMMMMMMMMM

* *
*

(1) The Hebrew word *Ur* means literally "flame" or "light." Ur is the name of an ancient city in Sumer and the tone of Uriel the Archangel. *Uriel* translates "God is Light" and the *Urim* and the *Thummim* worn by the high priest of Israel translate as "Lights" and "Perfections." The city of Ur was located in Mesopotamia (present-day Iraq) on the Euphrates River near the head of the Persian Gulf. According to Genesis, Abraham (an embodiment of El Morya, c. 2100 B.C.) left Ur of the Chaldees to go into the land of Canaan. In the twenty-first and twenty-second centuries B.C., Ur was a flourishing cultural, political and economic center. El Morya has revealed that in his life as Abraham, he was a native of Nippur, Sumer's cultural and religious center, where his father Terah, whose pagan religion he challenged, was a temple priest. (2) Hermes Trismegistus is an Ascended Master who was known to the ancient Egyptians and Greeks as the great philosopher, priest and king who authored sacred writings and alchemical and astrological works.

8

Ashram Notes

From the fragment of the OM-Light that is within us all, I salute you! Yet even my personality joyfully greets your personality; for as there is the Inner Light, so there is a Light that is externalized.

The Ascended Masters who hover in spiral formation above us are motivated by the highest God-Good to create a thoughtform of Beauty, a thought-form of Life, a thoughtform of the Divine Will to magnetize our souls to the plane of the Christ.

Even so, may we all lift up our souls into his Sacred Heart this Christmas Eve. For it is the will of God that all of his sons and daughters enter into the essence of the divine spark that they might be raised to Godhood through the mastery of the inner as well as the outer self.

Hierarchy awaits the coming of the children. They shall come singing, garlands of flowers in their arms. They shall come with the awareness of their humble estate and their littleness, yet joying in the knowledge of the infinite power and glory of the All-Father hidden in the divine majesty of their souls.

The mountains tremble and the light of the morning sends its splendor to the heart at this Christmas season. While pierced with the radiance of the Divine Mother, we approach the timeless regions of the sun center of being, where we constantly maintain the joy of our union with Christ.

Great is my happiness to tell you of a dispensation granted us. Each of you who has served as a contact for the Ashram is now called upon to be a focal point for a circle of up to 9 contactees—worthy souls who will make up your group.

Each of you will relay the Ashram Notes and rituals to your circle of 9 from the present source. In due time each of the 9 will call another circle of 9, multiplying our numbers to 81; and again, each of the 81 will call their circle of 9, increasing our meditation powers to 729.

Thus shall the Light of the Ashram cover the earth. Each link shall maintain the sacredness of the contact with one another and with the source. And thus shall we strive to establish and strengthen our personal moorings in God through our individual oneness with the Almighty I AM Presence.

The Ashram will hold a special convocation from 11:00 to 11:30 p.m. on Christmas Eve. We invite all contacts to joyously participate at that hour in our communion in the birth of Christ in all hearts and in our souls' ascent to the plane of the avatars.

Our goals through the coming year will be to bring about great spiritual advancement in all children of the Light, and in ourselves emergence from all negative karma into a positive soul-givingness.

To that end we call forth the blessing of the sacred orders and their members, from the neophytes to the initiates, and we pledge our complete obedience to the Great White Brotherhood and our oneness with its aims.

Peace in the living Christ.

Blessings,

Mark

Ashram Notes

The Lord Maitreya asks all in my Ashram to devote a special service on behalf of those in mental hospitals who are in various states of mental illness — whose tortured and tormented beings cry out for deliverance.

Maitreya also asks you to direct the Light of our Ashram to all who are suffering from severe accidents and loss of family members through untimely deaths.

Send vibrations of God's healing harmony, his healing peace and his healing protection to these — in great power.

The Buddha saith, "Bind up the world's wounds. So shall I mend the chalice of my ministering servants...and Christ shall fill it with Light."

Sanctē,

M.

Ashram Notes

And now I would speak of sendings...

What stainless beauty is in Christ!

Such a vibration appropriated by the devotee can cleanse the soul whiter than snow, whiter indeed than any fuller on earth could white it. What refinement of the spirit is in this sending from the aura purified—

Ah, the stainless beauty of Christ!

Change into Light the vibrations you call Darkness. Let joy displace all sorrow. Sleepy minds will awaken to spiritual alertness through the divine alchemy.

Yes, yes, from the All let fly through you arrows of transmutation; and the dark arrows shall not pass into your orbit. And the Light of your sendings shall return to cloak you in a cloud of ethereal radiance.

Consider the unselfish joy you create through your meditation rituals, the countless hearts you vivify and warm, O my Suns. Let your sendings ever be my rays directed to the subtle bodies of other Suns. Let them be for their awakening, to transmute, to bless and to create the Good and the Beautiful.

So shall you all come together in an ordered haven, and you shall build a tower and you shall merge your lights as one—a Lighthouse to many in need. And you shall do my will as it is the will of God, for this shall be your desiring. And the Eternal Guru shall teach you, being not removed from you but close at hand, close at heart.

The glory of the Nativity is the glory of recreation. "Behold, I make all things new!" Recreation is the making new of that which was corrupted from the Creation. For the Adam may die, but the new man in Christ is ever making himself alive. And the glory of the resurrection is the order of the new birth.

This pattern of self-regeneration, experienced again and again through Christ, is indispensable to the New Age. Therefore, tune your joy always to the Nativity as well as to your rebirth in the risen Christ. But take care in your soul's cyclic rounds through the ritual of recreation that you intensify God's love in your heart.

May the chorusings of angels be close to you during Advent and in the holy days of the Christ Mass to come. For these remind you of and link you to God's message of peace and goodwill through the Christ Child.

Remember the Messenger and the Sender, even as you forget not the message or the sending. And be ye also messengers and senders. Increase the consciousness of the living Flame within you, destroy your finite delusions, and let us mightily send one another the message of our immortality.

A ship shall approach the haven laden with treasures; its salvation is in your ancient sendings.

Remember the hands clasped from higher to lower. Remember that the lowest is thus linked to the highest—and the one who sits on the right hand of God clasps the Father's hand.

Remember the Brotherhood; be outposts of its sendings. Work, worship and plan, that the highest good may come by your presence among men. Be unceasing.

The Lord's song be with you.

Eternal blessings,

11

Ashram Notes

Let wisdom from the mountain fall upon the plain, that good fruit come to harvest.

The laws the Crossbearer expounded upon have influenced humanity, but O how many of those laws have been ignored!

And Light has not penetrated the Darkness that has covered the earth, for the walls of self-imposed ignorance have interfered—by free will. And therefore gross darkness has covered the people.

But the LORD shall arise upon thee, and his glory shall be seen upon those who worship the Light, who appropriate the Light—by free will.

Some among the God-seekers fear the contamination of their auras. They tremble lest they be defiled. On personal contact and even through clairvoyance they analyze the subtle bodies of one another.

Yet in the sending out of the radiance of Love is the most perfect of antiseptics; and even fear may be healed by this Love. For oneness with the Creator is the most purifying of all rays. And he holds the universe in his hand while Darkness still trembles there mixed with Light.

Is the servant greater than his Lord?

Show compassion and understanding to one another even in your weaknesses, for so shall one and all gain strength. And your oneness with the downtrodden through Christ's compassion and understanding shall be as a samadhi,* greater than the samadhi of a thousand yogis who are without this union.

Strength is born of weakness moving toward perfection, and each overcoming is a step on the way. Joy comes to those who have overcome sorrow; and those who have walked in Darkness shall love Light more.

Your auras shall grow to a fuller embodiment of the Father as you breathe thoughtforms of holiness even into the unholy in yourself and your brother. Transmutation is a coal from the altar of heaven fanned aflame by your perception of the need to burn away the dross from your own eye that the mote in thy brother's eye be also burned away—by the alchemical fires of Love.

Cleave to me. For even the leper will not defile you as you cleave to me. This Ashram stands before dawn as a tower rising in the night, waiting to greet the first ray. Hinder not the will of God through ignorance, even while you seem to be wise and feel yourself nestled in the bosom of Truth.

Even the mighty gain strength in humility as they stand before me. And how truly have I exalted them of low degree while bringing down the mighty from their seats.

*samadhi [Sanskrit, literally "putting together," "uniting"]: in Hinduism, a state of profound concentration or absorption resulting in perfect union with God; the highest state of yoga. In Buddhism, samadhis are numerous modes of concentration believed to ultimately result in higher spiritual powers and the attainment of enlightenment, or nirvana.

Bind one another's wounds, heal one another's afflictions, and breathe gentle kindness into the spirits of the downtrodden. So shall the spirit of the Cross-bearer fill this worldwide Ashram.

And the love cup of the universe shall pour the oil of the Spirit upon us. And in its trembling shall arise a work in this day that you have not begun to conceive of even in your dreams.

My love calls . . . and the Presence of the LORD shall arise upon thee, and his glory shall be seen upon thee.

12

Ashram Notes

My Beloved,

Through the night keep thy hand fast in mine.

Avoid the sin of cynicism. See beauty, beauty, beauty even in ashes—for from death and decay new life shall arise. The puny monad on a dying world shall expand the consciousness to encompass the ever-living cosmos.

What beautiful linkages of pure hearts are established through the soul who is not blinded by form, whose thoughts lurk not in the muddy clay of race or in the limitation of creed.

Those who are of the earth, earthy are like small boys who throw stones in the ocean saying, "By and by we shall cross over on this bridge of stones."

Let them place their hands in the hand of the Infinite. So shall they fly through the Inner Light and the God within to a blissful crossing!

Take courage, take care. Be a doer of all that is good and plant the seed of kindness in the heart of your neighbor. Be not overcome of the spoilers, for they are but broken souls who are overcome of a lack of self-control.

With a prayer on our lips let us breathe His name, that even the sinful may come to Him.

The Christ stands, while the spheres are crashing and crumbling, to call us one by one to his side. Let us steadfastly answer the Call with the highest in ourselves. Let us arise from the thought and the dark thoughts that say we cannot conquer.

Through him we shall conquer all worlds whatsoever. Let us fit ourselves for his little infinite band. We can indeed, as has been said, do all things through Christ who strengthens us hour by hour.

Strike a blow for the Lord. Remember the sword of the LORD and of Gideon. Break the pitchers if need be, but let the Light shine!

We shall lose our bodies in time except He redeem them. Let us take courage. Let us wait upon the LORD. Let us fight and renew our strength, fight and renew our strength. Let us mount up with wings as eagles, as the prophet said. Let us run and not be weary. Let us walk and not faint.

The fiat has gone out: May our Ashram glow with renewed Life and Light, and above all with Love as devotion from the heart!

Shake off the fetters of personality. Do not look for perfection in others until the perfection within yourself is shining fully without.

Eternal blessings,

Ashram Notes

Beloved,

This Ashram Note takes the form of a prayer for departing loved ones, that you might be comforted in time of bereavement and that you might comfort others through the intercession of the angelic hosts. Use it with the certain knowledge and the profound faith that the call to Almighty Light, the Father-Mother God, on behalf of those close to you and the many who are making their way across samsara to the Eternal Bourne, *is always answered!*

A Prayer for Souls Who Are Taking Their Leave of the Earth Today

Beloved Presence of God I AM in the hearts of all mankind, beloved Lord Michael, Archangel of Deliverance, and your angelic hosts:

In the name of the souls of humanity— particularly those who shall be called from their mortal forms by our heavenly Father this day— I make this call.

Let the angels of peace stand by the physical body of each soul and hold at perfect peace the aura and feelings of these ones taking their leave of the physical octave and of those present where such release is taking place.

Through the presence of the seraphim of God let the aura of sanctity be sustained at the solemn hour of transition that the soul may be cut free from her earthly tabernacle by the legions of the Archangels Michael, Gabriel, Raphael and Uriel.

Let all fear and doubt, sorrow in separation and grief in the parting of loved ones be consumed by Archangel Zadkiel's angels of the violet flame that there be no distress to souls standing at the threshold of a new freedom.

Let the LORD's angels of deliverance meet each soul. Let not a lifestream belonging to earth's evolution pass through the veil of so-called death unattended.

According to his will, let all children of God who pass from the screen of life this day be taken to the temples of mercy and forgiveness and bathed in the purifying fires of Saint Germain's violet flame.

Let them be prepared to pass before the Lords of Karma in the dignity of their Christ Self and in full conscious awareness; and let each one be assigned to a schoolroom of Life and be given the opportunity to study the Great Law as it pertains to his own evolution.

I call to the Lords of Mercy and Love to enfold all those whose loved ones are about to leave or are recently departed this earth, to transmute and consume all burden and sense of loss, and to fill each heart and home with peace and understanding for the opportunity afforded souls called to other realms to progress on the path of eternal Life.

So be it! I accept it done in the name of our Lord and Saviour Jesus Christ, Amen.

Ashram Notes

This Ashram Note contains some miscellaneous thoughts on my soul's approach to God. May you benefit from them and from giving the mantrams of Jesus that echo in our hearts.

Blessings always,

Mark

THE QUEST

Seek and you shall find. If he cry not, even the child will not be fed his mother's milk. The demand must be created if the supply is to be forthcoming.

You must first feel it within yourself. You must first yearn for it, burn for it. You must create the vacuum within yourself if you are to be filled.

If you work, burn, and yearn for it, I say you will get it—the Guru. The minute you create the desire, no one can withhold from you the fulfillment of that desire—not even the Guru.

THE UNITY

Christianity when it accomplishes its purpose is unity between soul and God. Worship is based solely upon the knowledge of the I and the Thou—that he is my Lord and that I am his servant. But for the man who knows that everything is God, including himself, there is no I, no Thou, neither worship nor religion.

He is become one with the One.

It is not I doing anything but He is doing it. I am feeling the hand of God all the time in the word and the work. Always keep this thought before you: It is not I, the talker, the doer; it is the Eternal One, God, expressing himself through me. And I affirm that the "I AM" in me is that One. God in me is the All.

Let no man take the thought into his head that he is great. Only God is Great. People think they are the doers. Only God is the Doer. Some don't know that the Divine Omnipotence is simply using us as his instruments.

If we have great ideas, we shall do great works. If we have the mind of Christ, we shall do Christlike works. In fact, we shall do Christ's work on earth.

It is not the I doing it and it is not the Thou. It is the "I-Thou" that is in me. It is the Father and the Son doing it in me. It is the Father-Son who have taken up their abode in me.

I am the Thou and I am the I. I know the duality of myself through the All-in-all. I am the cup and the contents of Omniscient Being. Yet, I am nothing.

O my beloved Jesus, Thou art the Everything, I am the Nothing!

86

THE RENUNCIATION

Make no condition with God concerning what he shall do and what he shall not do. Be true to your inner nature and leave the results unconditionally in his hands. This is true renunciation. It saves you all the worries and all the cares. This is belief in the Divine Law of God, which never disappoints. This is indeed true renunciation.

A man who knows through divine knowledge that he and God are one will live up to that. A man who knows that the world is false and that the only real thing in the world is himself, as a free agent of the Almighty—that man will encompass the world with his heart and endue all whom he meets with the same self-knowledge.

Your right is only to action. Pray that you be God in action always. Then do the very best that you can and leave the results in God's hands.

We are all instruments of God. He is doing all things. The greatness of man and woman is the greatness of God, as they are the expressions of that eternal energy.

THE MANTRAMS

Meditate daily on these mantrams of Jesus until their recitation in your heart and mind (and aloud when you are alone) becomes a mighty momentum for right action—righteousness in God's name!

1. I and my Father are one!*
2. I can of mine own self do nothing.
   It is the Father in me which doeth the work!*
3. My Father worketh hitherto and I work!*
4. I must work the works of Him that sent me!*
5. I will work while I have the Light [the Guru] with me, for the night cometh [the absence of the Guru] when no man can work!*

*Give this mantram 9 times or in multiples of 27 up to 108.

Ashram Notes

Tonight you are in my heart. All the centuries are bound within that timeless region.

Bursting with compassion, I yearn to see all of us who are children of God's heart fulfill our highest destiny, both in our private lives and in our work with the Brotherhood.

The Brotherhood sendeth peace and greetings to you all—impersonally, as the sun shineth on the just and the unjust, yet personally, as the honeybee caresseth each flower.

It goes without saying, and you know, that the Ashram was created neither for personal motive nor for personal gain. Our labors are of Love and for Love, directed to every heart crying out to God in need.

We live to bring the knowledge and the vibration of the higher powers to men and nations—even to those who know us not on the outer but know us on the inner—through the Ashram's spiritual outposts everywhere. Thus we would build foundations of personal godliness within ourselves and in all our contacts so that by the forging of individual God-links the planet might be redeemed.

Recently permission was granted from the Darjeeling Council for us to expand the Ashram. This sponsorship is an example of the unselfed love of the Brotherhood to the end that untold numbers of souls might join in our labors for the unity of the spiritually minded of the nations.

This is to be accomplished with a minimum increase of our duties and a maximum increase of our attunement, with a net gain of planetary benefits. The linking of our meditation rituals person to person across the miles will create a planetary net of Divine Love covering many geographical areas of time and space with the Light of our sendings.

The garments of the Mother of the World weave a higher gateway for all...

It was not our intention in announcing this opportunity to unnecessarily burden any of our contacts but to give you the vision of the multiplication of hearts through our mutual efforts.

Dear hearts, you do not need to secure the cooperation of nine souls all at once. Even our group, at seven, is still short two souls. You may start with one or two and build to the desired strength. For in the nine is the power of the three-times-three.

Call for these souls and the Spirit will send them.

The secretary of our group stands ready to help you and will lend you a set of forms for you to copy in the correct order. You do not need a typewriter, for a hectograph or carbon paper and pencil or ballpoint pen applied with steady hand and heart will do to reproduce the required rituals.

The letters may be mailed out as you are able. We suggest every week for the first three weeks and after that every two weeks. Make no firm rule, but serve as your time permits. However, we do want you to forward our occasional Ashram Notes to Morya's chelas as soon as possible.

In short, we ask that you make the effort to find one or two in your circle of fellow students of Christ's mysteries who would welcome the opportunity to engage in the Light-sendings of the Ashram.

We suggest you tell them you have been fortunate enough to make a good and reliable contact with Hierarchy and you want them to have the opportunity to take part in a meditation group you have been called upon to start for the blessing of humanity and the raising of the vibrations of the planet. Tell them their participation will result in their individual spiritual growth as well as their oneness with the Ascended Masters.

We ask each of you to send the small amount necessary for paper and postage to our secretary. This request does not come from us but is a requirement of the karmic law, that as we have freely received the words and the blessing of the Master M., we may now freely give of ourselves to maintain the Ashram. Thus in due time it may manifest outwardly for all Light-bearers to see, whether in this century or another.

The groundwork must be laid.

Our hearts are somewhat troubled in our labors because some of you have not acknowledged our recent communications. We realize the burdens that each of you carries, but we do ask you to set aside just the few minutes each day that are needed for this vital work.

My brethren, it pains me to speak in this wise, as I have not done so previously; but of necessity the burden of the LORD is laid upon me. I ask you therefore in the name and the love of the Father that you lay this matter to your heart and make the physical contacts we request now and then. It is not that I am not aware of your love, it is just that the Law ordains the response and the expression of gratitude from each one, rendering like service for service given.

The faithful who have labored with me manage to find the little time that is needed to spread the work of the Master to the glory and praise of thy God forever and ever. We ask you to also respond to our call especially on behalf of those who would love to participate in these meditation rituals.

In closing we pray: "Father, we visualize a closer link between each one who is a part of the building of the worldwide structure of the Ashram; we see one and all knit together solely through the Christ image reflected in all its glory within our souls. Help us to be your hands and feet here on earth, making your vision a reality every day."

Blessings and love eternally,

Mark

Written after the Nine O'Clock Meditation
January 20, 1954

16

Ashram Notes

The enclosed flower is to remind you of your soul's daily unfoldment through our Ashram work. One has been sent to each member after having remained for a number of days before the picture of the Blessed Mother on the Master's altar.

These flowers were blessed by God and all who attended our bimonthly meditation; to theirs I add my humble blessing.

May I suggest that you keep your flower on your altar to remind you of us who love you, of the Master M. and of the oneness of our souls in our meditation rituals. Sometimes you may choose to wear your flower, bringing its joy to others.

The opened flower represents the Spirit of the LORD blossoming throughout the world in all God's children—perfect, beautiful, radiant, divine and unaffected by the storms of egos.

The bud represents the potential of your True Self. Yours is to follow the spiral of its opening in your heart.

Though of paper, this little flower exudes the aura of the soul. It is charged with our Mother Mary's love and needs no other fragrance.

Mark

17

Ashram Notes

This message was recorded for three members of the Ashram who recently met in one of our eastern cities. We offer it herewith for your edification and blessing.

When the fingers of God lighted the flame in my lantern borne earthward, it was with purpose. And it was a living memorial to the night we saw His star in the East.

Join your heart with mine to Christ in the temple of all lives. Ours is union—union with God, yes—and the forging of a holy link with one another as we bring men of goodwill to God. Deep, loving attention is needed to fulfill the eternal purpose.

Neglect not the mantrams nor the work. The day shall reveal itself. The night is past at dawn; but comes the afternoon! Therefore in your zenith and brightness lay hold on God on behalf of all people, ere night fall.

Weave a chain of beautiful thoughts like fragrant flowers in a lei. Send them to all who are the living but offer them especially to the saints.

Observe how men raise up memorials to the dead, and observe the carnage that is the bitter fruit of their hostility.

Fields of war and carnal strife remain as repositories of the struggle of human hatred and the malice of mortals. These records piled layer upon layer, as the centuries of man's inhumanity to man move on, bind the race to their enslavement under the gods of war and their cult of death.

But you, O beloved, have come to endow every bush and tree with your love as a memorial to Hierarchy, to the Magi and, yes, by God's will to the littlest child in whom his love shines.

Days gone by have shown the need for questioning the origins of thought. You know that good thoughts originate from your souls. But do you know that evil thoughts do not originate from your souls? Since they do not and they are not of you, you need to get rid of them by the fastest and best means.

The best warfare against evil thoughts is to challenge them with the sacred word of Truth and to replace them with Truth's wise dominion over every thought and feeling. Then pay them no mind and mightily raise your consciousness to the Creator, whose crystal-pure thoughts we find frozen as flowers and snowflakes and captured in the splendor of rainbows and the wings of birds.

Join me now in the most important work of our Ashram! This is the Call and the calling to that work:

The Call from Hierarchy

A call is sent forth from the highest watch-tower on Terra to the watchmen on the wall of the LORD.

It is a call to all brotherhoods and sister-hoods that conform to the original esoteric and moral standards of Christ but that for want of the pristine teachings of God have not applied the founding principles of Christianity in their orders.

You have a mighty work to do and you are needed as links in the chain of Hierarchy. But you cannot work a work in this day while your souls lie dormant in your ignorance of our Lord's true message.

Therefore we proclaim to you that the Lord has empowered us to reactivate the founding flame of all spiritual orders as well as the endowing dispensations of human institutions.

We invite all world servers to join us in bringing to new birth the greatest spiritual awareness and revival of the Lord's ministry preceding the New Age of Aquarius.

We resolve, therefore, to support the true devotees of Light and Truth who will rally to new heights of God's consciousness to the end that all children of God may rapidly mature to their rightful place on the path of discipleship unto Christ.

Let it be so, that keystones might be placed in the arches of the temple invisible who will assist the Cosmic Christ in bringing in God's kingdom on earth and the Hierarchy in fulfilling their mission of Love.

Decree with me tonight in the Mind of Christ and in the Presence of the exalted ones, who are one with our Divine Mother! Tread the wind and the wave, as the eagle flies to heights undreamed of. Avoid the flowing lava of karma.

Above all credos rises thy one Love, which thou must now direct to all humanity. For only the Love that thou givest is the Love that thou mayest keep.

In the consciousness of the Divine Manchild, we invoke the Christ Spirit in the precious infants held in the loving arms of the Mother Divine.

Awake!

Reflect Christ.

Reflect the Holy Purpose.

Reflect God.

Burn delusion. Live in Truth.

We raise the sacred chalice.

Fill it with thy Love.

18

Ashram Notes

When the darkest spectre of failure looms, keep your thoughts aspiring toward the highest Love. Remember the exactness of the Law even when you forget this Love!

Speaking of retribution, again the Law whispers: Why enmesh yourself in vengeance? Does not the Law compensate? Lift upward a prayer for the fallen. So shall you leap toward the stature of the Crossbearer.

Love is our substance, the woven and the interwoven. From this fabric emerge good and bad dreams according to thy free will of design-desire.

Penetrate and cognize the substance of thy designing and thy desiring; so shalt thou come to the house of Light where Darkness is not.

Time becomes a benediction when the hand of the Creator is ever remembered; space becomes a blessing when his Spirit is embraced. Struggle with me through the mud of karma to Jordan's waters. The birds fly above the mud, and the sun drieth and purifieth all.

All things work together for the Good unto those who truly love the Good, "to them who are the called according to his purpose," as my brother Paul said.

Eternal blessings,

19

Ashram Notes

It is not without reason that I advocate the development of a worldwide consciousness of the Good; for it is not only the world that benefits from this right-mind-ful-ness but also ourselves. Yet one must think in terms of giving rather than merely receiving the fruits of the Mind of God.

You have heard it said, "It is more blessed to give than to receive." Prove the LORD now herewith by attuning your soul to the higher tensions.

Our work must relieve world tensions of the wrong sort and bring about creative tensions of the right sort. The yearnings and the strivings of the human heart for the Good and for the Mind of God, which was in Christ Jesus, must be generated and regenerated by our Ashram meditations and rituals.

Remember always that it is the LORD, the I AM THAT I AM, who is the Doer. Be content to be an unseen channel for his Presence.

There are those among us who watch over you always. For example, one of us, a devotee of Christ, received word through this channel concerning certain natural disturbances anticipated in America in the coming season. These karmic effects were somewhat mitigated through the oneness of our love and our work.

Storms, floods and violent upheavals in Nature are ever the result of man-made causes. Karma. Humanity would smile at this yet they themselves have not taken corrective measures. As I speak, the seeds of karma continue to sprout; and mankind know not a better way—yet they will not listen.

A high and holy charge shall be given to you for the coming days. Watch for it. Pray for it.

It is the unified work to elevate the religious thought of East and West. Each of us is given responsibility and to all of us is conferred a message of Love. Let us build a great pool of Love, enough for the whole world, enough to smother the flames of all mayic hate of the human heart.

Think often of the Lord's words "Lo, I AM with you alway, even unto the end of the [Piscean] age," and of the deeper meaning: "Lo, the I AM THAT I AM of me—the Presence of the Son of God who I AM—is with you alway, even to the end of the cycles of your karma on earth."

When seeing the Divine Mother at work in Nature and especially in springtime, it is easy to understand why the ancients called her Mother Nature. Most people can enjoy the beauty of Nature; yet she has few devotees who can see her real beauty in the Spirit that endures behind the crumbling walls of time.

Please understand that the personal attention we give to our chelas is not to elevate the lesser self nor to slight the Real Self of those who make up this Ashram. For we are all interested in building a better race spiritually, mentally and even materially. And we know that the Good that comes to the one is for the blessing of all.

I comment on this so that you will be able to see the great love for all souls behind the purposes of the King of kings, in whose peace we labor.

In our Ashram I advocate the cultivation of efficiency as long as it does not stifle the development of the soul. So, in the interest of efficiency these Ashram Notes are simply written. Often they are dictated with the needs of a particular individual or group in mind.

In this vein, I ask you to take to heart that this channel needs to hear from you concerning your spiritual progress so that he can respond to your needs and those of your group in a practical way. So please drop us a line once a month and let us know how you are doing. Your kind thoughts are always there, but we would appreciate a direct word from time to time.

At night let your soul sleep in God. Abide in the courts of Shamballa. Rest neath the stars as you send rays of peace to brothers and sisters caught in the maelstrom of their returning karma. That they might know the better way is our prayer.

Eternal blessings,

20

Ashram Notes

The illumination of the inner nature produces the desire for that perfection which your soul cries out for in its most intense longing. Even so, the contemplation of the life of Jesus Christ often evokes the radiant desire for the purity of purpose he manifested.

To want to be a burning brand spelling out Christ's holiest patterns on the lives of countless millions is a pure and noble desire.

But who is ready to open the door to the Great Initiator who comes to initiate the aspiring one? Who is ready to receive the burning brand unto himself for the transfiguration of his own human nature that is the prerequisite to the accomplishment of the goal?

The mind entertains itself with ideas of spiritual greatness; but the angel of illumination who comes with flaming sword is denied entrance to the precincts of the soul by the earthly ego.

By turns the ego is caught up in the ecstasy of a self-transfiguration and plunged headlong into the despondency of a self-annihilation. But these extremes will vanish forever as the soul passes from death's tomb to the chamber of the Resurrection Spirit.

The angel of the resurrection draws nigh the earth today, desiring to breathe into man's nostrils the same holy breath of the second birth that was breathed into the nostrils of Jesus Christ two thousand years ago.

Countless elementals of the Nature kingdom have devoted themselves in pure love to the service of mankind throughout the aeons; their activities have often prevented cataclysmic destruction to the world.

Remember therefore the service to life rendered by the unknown and unseen Nature spirits under the direction of their hierarchs and Elohim, who are indeed cosmic servants.

If the precious salamanders, sylphs, gnomes and undines gladly do the will of God (which by all means they naturally do), then can you, whom the Father endowed with the potential for Christhood, give any less than Christ's loving service to all life through your meditation rituals, regardless of whether or not you receive recognition for a labor well done?

Accept now through the open door of this glorious Eastertide the outpouring of the Lord's Spirit and the resurrection fires from the angels of the resurrection. And let the true illumination of the inner nature melt the discordant elements of self-ignorance within your world.

Then shall you become a veritable burning brand in the hand of God delivering the fiery baptism of the Holy Comforter to all who are called to witness at the tomb to the victory of eternal Life over Death and Hell.

It is my hope that the increased activity of the lifestreams who are in contact with me through these

Ashram Notes and through my ray, which I direct personally to each one, will accelerate the world tempo of true spirituality in the coming days, when Christians turn their attention to Christ's Passion.

It is our prayer that the pulsations of your meditations and affirmations of the Good and the Beautiful may serve to intensify and anchor the holy vibrations of the Body and Blood of Christ in the lives of countless souls who look to him for their redemption.

Dwell in faith and in the certain knowledge that it is the will of God that you accept the fire of his transfiguring Spirit for the transfiguration of your own so that you may serve as his instrument.

Let the Father of Lights, even the Ancient of Days, pour transfiguration's flame through every atom of your being until, drenched through and through by the holiness of God, you freely give to all souls of Light everywhere what you have freely received—the transfiguring power of the resurrection!

Eternal blessings,

Morya El

21

Ashram Notes

Along the lines of the impractical, some who call themselves students of esotericism pursue an intellectual God, making their intellect their god. As wizened wizards with heads in clouds of unknowing, they have not a drop of practical spirituality to offer the rising chela. And they themselves do not rise.

Along the lines of the practical, the chela who ponders the practicality of the Spirit will become wise indeed, for he will learn of the present opportunity to seek and find oneness with his God Presence. Oneness with God is the key to rising. All else can be set aside as nonessential fluff. Thus on wings of practicality the one-pointed chela shall rise!

Why is rising so important? People have said, "The sun also rises," "He is risen," "You will rise again," "He ascended into heaven." Sages tell their disciples to raise their vibrations. Little boys dream of flying airplanes and soaring across the sky like birds. And the scriptures say, "They that wait upon the LORD. . .shall mount up with wings as eagles."

Surely all this upward aspiration denotes that the soul must also rise. Therefore lift up thine eyes unto the hills, whence cometh thy help. For, as the

Psalmist sang, thy help cometh from the LORD, the I AM THAT I AM, which made heaven and earth.

Every soul that lifts up herself to God is lifting herself up to the Image and Likeness of God in which she was made. This pattern in the heavens—out of which God created the living soul and draped her with his mind and form and individuality—is held in the heart of the Christ, the same yesterday and today and forever.

And Elohim did create wonderfully and beautifully out of the original fiat and fohat* of the Creator. "So God created man in his own image, in the image of God created he him; male and female created he them. And God blessed them, and God said unto them, Be fruitful, and multiply, and replenish the earth, and subdue it.... And God saw every thing that he had made, and, behold, it was very good."

By and by man and woman lowered their gaze; and in so doing they lowered their vibration and locked into the energy veil called *e-veil.* And the mirage (i.e., the mirror image) of relative good and evil became the inversion of the Divine Image. And the patterns of the earth, earthy and of the astral plane polluted and perverted the heavenly patterns.

Alas, by subtle gradations of the mind and machinations of the Serpent class of fallen angels, tens upon tens of thousands of God's children fell from their divine dignity and its protective canopy.

This was "the Fall" in consciousness, in vibration, and in word and deed on the part of sons and

---

fohat: concentration of sacred fire, the creative Light/Energy that is released in response to the spoken Word; the mysterious electric power of Cosmic Consciousness, the impelling vital force, which when called into action by divine fiat, moves the evolutions of a universe, a galactic or solar system, or a single human being from the beginning to the completion of a mission.

daughters of God, which began when they, lured by devils' diversions, took their attention and their loving adoration from the God Presence. With the loss of their souls' self-knowledge and pristine purity came the necessity for twin flames to rise again to the plane of First Cause and to the point of origin: in the Beginning with the Word in Brahman.

In this thought of upliftment lies the secret of salvation, soul by soul and universally manifest. So the strong eye beholds God's presence and design in a radiant fire-pattern superimposed over everything visible and invisible. This clear seeing assists the fohatic forces in redeeming every lifestream, not the least one's own. Even so does the loving eye raise each child of the Light it seals into a focus of eternal Life and Truth and Love from God's heart.

Yes, by beholding and holding the immaculate matrix for every part of Life, which is God, you will become aware, softly, of a fragment of God's beauty within your own heart temple. And for you the joy of the day's labor and the day's rituals of devotion will evermore be to fan this flame of beauty into abundant activity.

You will be serene in the knowledge that as beauty rises and pulsates from your heart's altar, Love's victory rises with it. For your mind will be lit with freedom's torch and it will sense the beatification wrought by alchemical change even in the body's cells and atoms.

Though this change may not be noted by men, it will surely be recorded on the scrolls kept in the kingdom of God. And you will notice the change in yourself in that you are nonrecordant of vibrations of criticism, gossip and malignity. These simply cannot attach themselves to you, for the nuclei of Light in the body of the Christed one repel them.

Thus spinning in your suns, you may hold within God's earthly creation the heavenly pattern of Divine Love's perfection. And by reflection you obey our Lord's mandate "Be ye therefore perfect [on earth], even as your Father which is in heaven is perfect."

Great is the need, dear hearts, for chelas who will see the beauty within and who, by the mirror of their souls, will magnify it in God's name. These work out their salvation in the Light of the dawn and send forth at dusk to each child of God's heart the silent benediction of his flames.

Beware of the snares of the fallen ones who have crept unnoticed into the outer orders that in the past we Brothers have instituted through our work with various lifestreams. By subtlety and false teaching, some organizations we sponsored have fallen from the standards we set, retaining esoteric authority in name only.

Their present leadership would bind you by false fears. While mouthing the ancient precepts whose truth is timeless, these personalities who direct the physical plant today are not counted among the illumined ones. Theirs is a sort of dull glory, a dim and dusty reflection of the former greatness of the founders who wore our mantle.

Use discrimination in examining that which projects itself as flawless porcelain but is no longer. For their cupboards have no cups without cracks to hold our vibration—there have been many a slip twixt the cup and the lip, you see. Today's perfunctories shun today's true messengers of our bands. Remember, your allegiance is to the God Presence and not to the human person.

We of the Brotherhood guide you gently by Love's wisdom, that you may abide forever in the Light of God, which never fails. This Light will lift you to a place of such peace and plenitude of holy precepts as you find in your divinest dreams. There you will know fellowship forever with the Brothers of the Ashram flame.

I AM victoriously in the Light,

Morya El

Ashram Notes

Owing to the recent earthquakes in the Aleutian chain, which are far more serious in their ramifications than realized by most mundane minds, I am calling the Ashram into emergency session.

The Notes have begun to go forth again to break a period of silence instituted by me in this endeavor.

Continue all rituals of the Ashram and establish regular periods of radiating Light from your heart to strengthen the net of Light we are weaving across the world. Prepare spiritually for a most powerful meditation from Good Friday through Easter, when certain conditions such as the Light of spring equinox multiplying the Light of our Lord's Passion can be utilized to good advantage for the expansion of the Mystical Body of God on earth.

The Light of God will not fail *you;* do not fail *it.* Act now as radiating centers to restore inner balance

N.B. There were 40 earthquakes measuring 5.0 or greater on the Richter scale between March 9 and March 14, 1957, centered south of the Aleutian Islands in Alaska. The first of this series, epicenter 60 miles south of Atka Island, measured 8.1 on the Richter scale and caused considerable damage. The other quakes in the series, which lasted throughout the month, caused no damage.

and harmony to our earth and the beings of the
Nature kingdom. I am pouring out understanding to
you; be channels for this needed work.

March 14, 1957

23

Ashram Notes

This Ashram Note is from the one you call Saint Mark, who is serving with us today as the amanuensis of our Ashram. His words of wisdom follow.

While the extolling of virtue is profitable to elevate the nature of man, lamentations serve to promote a sense of humility.

The prophet Jeremiah, humbled by YAHWEH and the people's rejection of his message, was wont to lament: "I am the man that hath seen affliction by the rod of his wrath. He hath led me, and brought me into Darkness but not into Light."

What greater virtue is there than that sacred fire which God has already sealed within us, and what greater cause for lamentation than its loss?

How often we ignore this inner fire while decrying the seeds of error we have sown in the past, thereby amplifying them by our attention, energy and lament.

Were we to consciously withdraw this attention, energy and lament from the seeds of error (which, in any case, can never bring release and freedom) and let the Holy Breath breathe upon the inner fire with a true quickening, we should soon escape the fruit of our erroneous sowings, leaving behind a funeral pyre of our past negations that we ourselves should build and ignite, working with the Holy Spirit.

As we turn our hearts to the resurrection of Jesus Christ this Eastertide, it is a time to meditate upon the significance of his example. Were we to forever think upon the roles he played scene after scene in the great drama of his life's mission without emulating his example, just letting him do it all for us, we would never attain our victory in the imitation of Christ.

And unless we follow him in the regeneration of our souls by delivering his word and doing his works with signs following, we will not put on the mantle of our own Christhood, wherewith we should put out the hellfires of damnation and despair.

For truly we must, if we ourselves would escape the grave, "put off the old man with his deeds," as Paul admonished, and "put on the new man, which is renewed in knowledge after the image of him that created him," for "Christ is all, and in all." Let grave and graveclothes be done away with—and all human habits that have shrouded and buried us in mortality!

We will have none of it, for Christ the Lord is risen in us *today!*

Now is the accepted time. Now is the day of salvation. The kingdom of heaven is at hand *for you* whenever you decide to open wide the door of your heart to the Holy Spirit, bidding him enter and allowing him to breathe the breath of life upon the divine spark until the threefold flame is reignited and the gift of embryonic God consciousness is yours to fan, and fan again, and fan again!

Ask for this and ye shall receive it. The Comforter will come. He will pour the comfort flame through your mind, your body and your spirit. He will raise your threefold nature into the Trinity of God's divinity within you.

The dross of density will the fire consume. Just let God's flame live in you and expand and expand and expand the Trinity of its Power, its Wisdom, its Love. Let the mutuality of your will and God's will sustain it. This *is* the highest cooperation of Father and Son, as Above, so below, through the agency of the Holy Spirit.

Hold the visualization of our Lord's resurrection victory taking place in every heart on earth while you give the mantrams attached to this Note for forty days from Ash Wednesday through Easter Sunday. If you will do this as a penance for the sins of the world, you will pay him the highest honor and you will reap the highest reward.

Better still if you will also honor him with the nightly meditation rituals of your choosing. For the power of the Word and the thought of the Word and the meditation of the Word is very great for the conversion of souls to Jesus' Sacred Heart.

Saint Peter often spoke to me of his profound regret for the weaknesses of the flesh. He told me that at first he did not realize the significance of Jesus' statement to him when his brother Andrew took him to meet Jesus and Jesus looked at him intently and said: "You are Simon son of John; you are to be called Cephas"—meaning Rock.

You too will regret, as every disciple eventually does, human weaknesses that outcrop in your service to the Lord. Yet, as you ponder the matter of

your human self coexisting with your Divine Self—
your humanity within your divinity, which was also
the twofold nature of Jesus Christ—God will make
clear to you many things, even as he did to Peter.

The Saviour will reveal himself to you in a near
and dear proximity. And he may even give you a new
name! This succoring of your soul by the Lord will
furnish you with the oil of spikenard for the preparation of the body temple that awaits the soul's resurrection through initiation with her Rabboni.

All the fullness of resurrection's glory awaits
your recognition of the Inner Christ—but *you* must
call it forth. *You* must overcome the unglorious sense
of human selfhood and enter the glorious sense of
Christ Selfhood. *You* must do the Father's will, whether
the human like it or not, for you can't take the human
with you when you go. But the soul *must* attain her
resurrection or the soul isn't going anywhere!

You must know that the treasure house of your
Causal Body houses your Mighty I AM Presence, the
Great God Self, who is stronger than a winged lion.
This thoughtform is the symbol of Saint Mark. To me
it is a sign of my hope in Christ my Saviour and in the
God Presence with me. Yet I know I must do my part.
And you must do your part.

And as we play our bit parts we discover a mutual
dependence as members of Christ's Body here on
earth. This doctrine of the Lord working in us and
through us seems controversial at times but it is hidden
in the mystery of the Father-Mother and the triune God.

I exhort all who read my words to remember the
numberless volumes that have been written, the end-
less prayers that have been uttered and the countless

lives that have been lived for the salvation of the souls of God. Truly this highway of our God and of the saints marching in cannot be said to be unmarked, for Saint Peter also affirmed to me that which was recorded in Hebrews:

> How shall we escape, if we neglect so great salvation, which at the first began to be spoken by the Lord, and was confirmed unto us by them that heard him,
> God also bearing them witness, both with signs and wonders, and with divers miracles, and gifts of the Holy Ghost, according to his own will?

My most divine message of evangelism is yet to be revealed, for it is locked in the ascension process itself—mine and yours. Remember, dear hearts, that after Jesus' resurrection the most glorious of all occurrences was the glory that took place on Bethany's hill, when a cloud received him out of their sight.

Throughout each year to come unto your victory in the Light, and especially during the Easter season, hold fast to this advice: Cease to look at death whether as your enemy or as your friend. Cease to plan for your death or for anyone else's death.

On behalf of all souls evolving on planet earth, concentrate the energies of your lifestream in the visualization of the winged lion of the redeemed self becoming one with the winged God Self. Hold the picture in your mind's eye of your soul's ascension unto the I AM THAT I AM.

Let the rays of the Divine Sun of your dazzling God Reality blaze forth from your chakras and your aura. And let the Sun rays of your heart blend with the Sun rays of

Helios and Vesta (the Father-Mother who keep resurrection's flame in the sun center of our solar system).

Activate resurrection's fires in the body temples of all on earth who serve the Lord, even as those fires were self-activated in the Sacred Heart of Jesus and multiplied by the Cosmic Christ overshadowing him two thousand years ago.

When reaching for the Most High God and the hand of your Elder Brother, remember that Hope joins hands with Constancy and that Effort will bear fruit!

Blessings forever and forever. And may the Divine Union in the company of saints, angelic hosts and Ascended Masters of the Father's kingdom be ours unto eternal life.

I AM your brother,

Mark

The message of my son, who labors in Christ's name, bears my blessing. My greetings to you with every new sunrise of your life.

Eternal blessings,

M.

Morya El

Easter Meditation Ritual
For Activating the Resurrection Spirit in All Hearts
(Holy Saturday 9:00 p.m. MST†)

I

Instruction:

Visualize the Sacred Heart of Jesus superimposed over your heart and the hearts of all sons and daughters of God and children of the Light.

See Resurrection's Flame in its mother-of-pearl radiance as shafts of Light emitting from the hearts of God's issue on earth going forth to encircle the earth in a swaddling garment of the Resurrection, a spiral of living flame, quickening all to return to the inner walk with God—as you give this mantram with the full fervor of your heart's love and concentration through the third eye:

Mantram:

**I AM the Resurrection and the Life
of God's inner fire in my heart
and in the hearts of all sons and daughters of God
through the Resurrection Victory of Jesus Christ
over Death and Hell!***

N.B. The Holy Saturday and Easter Sunday meditations were originally given on April 20 and 21, 1957.
†This ritual may be given any day of the year that you desire to celebrate the resurrection.
*Give this mantram 9 times or in multiples of 27 up to 108.

II

Instruction:

Now, turning to the image of our Blessed Mother Mary on your altar, visualize the Immaculate Heart of Mary super-imposed over your heart and the hearts of all sons and daughters of God and children of the Light. Give this mantram as you hold in mind and heart the strength of her immaculate concept of their perfection and protection. Use the visualization of the Resurrection Flame as outlined on the previous page.

Mantram:

In the Immaculate Heart of Mary I trust!*

Easter Meditation Ritual

(Easter Sunday 10:00 a.m. or 10:00 p.m. MST)

"The Unison Ritual"

I

Instruction:

As you visualize beloved Jesus placing his Christ Presence over you and as you simultaneously pour forth your love to him and to your own Christ Presence, drawing the Beloved into your heart, soul, body, mind and spirit, give this fiat 9 times or in multiples of 27 up to 108:

**Christ the Lord is risen today
within my heart, my soul, my body,
my mind and my spirit!**

---

*Give this mantram 9 times or in multiples of 27 up to 108.

24

Ashram Notes

As the day ends, sweetness fills the mind that is aware, satisfied in a perfection outpictured, shining from the portal of the dawn unto the setting of the sun.

Children of my heart, contemplate the meaning of the "Everlasting Gospel." Contemplate the meaning of "Wheresoever this gospel shall be preached throughout the whole world, this also that she hath done shall be spoken of for a memorial of her."

The transformed Magdalene, out of whom Christ Jesus our Lord cast seven devils, outpictures the forgiveness and the sweetness of the prophecy "Though your sins be as scarlet, they shall be as white as snow; though they be red like crimson, they shall be as wool."

The Lords of Karma, in performing this whitening of the soul and her garments by the Christ Light of initiatic forgiveness, insist that her intent be to follow a path of self-perfectionment and goal-fitting.

Unless this intent be manifesting at least in embryo, the law of forgiveness will be nullified and the repetition of error will preclude man's freedom from sin. And man will be but a slave to his own desire-nature and the relentless attack upon the soul by the barbaric, untamed ego, against which even the best saints have had to wage war.

Progress is our watchword, and so John Bunyan was guided to bring forth a *Pilgrim's Progress*. May you, too, leave tyrannical Egoland and the dictatorship of King James (King Self-centeredness) for religious freedom in the Netherlands and beyond as you set fair sail on the Mayflower for the Promised Land.

Then from new shores may you make a declaration of independence from Egoland, founding in freedom's name a country where all the sons of Mary, "A-Mary-Ka," may flower under God.

Under the wings of the great eagle may you find shelter in the kingdom of heaven, the kingdom of the Spirit, as well as on earth that you may develop your divine nature as God intended you to do in peace and eternal helpfulness to the causes of Christ love and freedom.

The scales of life reveal the soul's infinite sensitivity to karma. The law of the circle guarantees to every man the justice he often decries saying, "There is no justice."

The Karmic Board tempers many a backlash of causes reaching into the world of effects to strike hammer blows on offending humanity. Truly, this quality of mercy is not strained!

Recall to mind the eternal truth that "one jot or one tittle shall in no wise pass from the law [of karma] till all be fulfilled." The law indeed demands repayment for every jot and tittle of the karma of human petulancy.

Therefore, if you would implore mercy for the human condition to mitigate the requirement of karmic law, remember Jesus' words and set your house in order before you submit your petition to heaven's court:

"If ye forgive men their trespasses, your heavenly Father will also forgive you: But if ye forgive not men their trespasses, neither will your Father forgive your trespasses."

It is the will of God, dear hearts, that everyone should permanently anchor himself in the spirit of instantaneous forgiveness. Beloved, you ought to radiate the spirit of forgiveness into all wrongs committed by or against you. For it is thus that the overpowering accumulations of human karma may be 'vaporized' into the ethereal Light and consumed by God's all-consuming fire; then the energies can be requalified by Love.

During these days I urge that the cup of your consciousness be extended to receive the blessings that the Brotherhood is sending into the world as a positive force. The Great Divine Director himself is literally pouring out his love to those who do the will of God.

I am looking forward to a show of hearts who will take their time and energy—being as serious about this business of their heavenly Father as they are about the mundane—to prepare the way for the highest transmittals of the Christ consciousness to the earth.

Will you not recognize, as did the author of *Julius Caesar,* that

> There is a tide in the affairs of men,
> Which, taken at the flood, leads on to fortune;
> Omitted, all the voyage of their life
> Is bound in shallows and in miseries.

On such a full sea are we now afloat,
And we must take the current when it serves,
Or lose our ventures.

Will you not recognize this flood tide of Light
that I send you and take it to inundate the earth with
Light and to deposit the gold of the pure hearts of our
Ashram co-workers at the feet of the Christ in all?

And these hearts, your hearts, can hold the
immaculate concept for every chela whom I count as
a member of my household. Refuse to accept as a
permanent part of their true self such outer failures as
are seen on the screen of maya; and then replace
those framed images with the true image of Christ's
victory shining beyond the years.

I am generating in you who sustain contact with
me through our meditation rituals a true quickening
into that holy will that shall enable you to overcome
both Death and Hell in this life and today.

Eternal blessings in God's will,

Morya El

April 4, 1957

25

Ashram Notes

Lord Maitreya desires that I convey his message to you.

Beloved Children,

The hours are preciously sustained for you—that you might occupy them stainless. I pray that your divine memory be opened by reason of God's laws so that you may once again enter the sweet communion of the kingdom of heaven, wherein we who are of the ascended hosts abide.

Somehow the veils of maya have hidden the melodies, the rare perfumes, the divine realities and the delicate hues of the heavenly kingdom from your consciousness so that they have seemed unreal and far off.

That memory's door may once again swing wide for you, I am come. That you may learn and earn once again the almost effortless, or magical, power of divine precipitation is my desire.

You labor long and hard to sustain yourselves, yet without your attention your bodies survive in safety each night through the Christ Presence, who silently watches over you during sleep and restores you to physical consciousness when you awaken.

Shall the Great God Self, who is your Real Self, fail you? This is impossible if you but learn to abide in the consciousness of the I AM Presence. Soon you will find that not only will the Presence not fail you, but you will not fail the Presence.

For this LORD, who is your Keeper, shall preserve your soul from all evil—the energy veil, the maya—of the astral plane. This Guardian of Israel shall preserve the going out and the coming in of your soul as you take your leave of the body at night to journey to Shamballa for our Light-sendings and then return at dawn to take up the day's karma.

"For thine is the kingdom, and the power, and the glory forever" refers to the three conditions of consciousness to which you may attain by abiding in the Christ Presence. Step by step you receive the initiations under Hierarchy of (1) the Holy Spirit (the kingdom), (2) the Father (the power), and (3) the Son (the glory).

As you enter the plane where I abide and relate it to yourself, so shall you also know your Presence. Contact with the office of the Cosmic Christ through your own Christ flame opens up the channels for continuous contact with the LORD God and the Brothers in white. These mentors of the Spirit are ever ready to assist you to always know the omnipresence of the kingdom (of the Holy Spirit), to always know the omnipotence of the power (of the Father) and to always know the omniscience of the glory (of the Son).

As the Hierarch who represents the Cosmic Christ to the people of this planet, I shed forth my

Light in countless ways. And today I am lowering my vibration to the level of the etheric plane in order that I might be very close to you, as close as heaven allows, that before I come nearer to humanity I may walk the earth through you—O preparing ones!

Therefore attune with me. Live in conscious awareness of my nearness. Be Love's doorway unto the children of the Light. Think of the kindness of God in giving life to you. Be grateful. Love the Spirit of the LORD, who, though formless, is bringing to you all form and beauty and grace and right-mind-fullness; and transform yourself in my Light, in my God Flame!

Now I am merging as one with the Spirit of the Resurrection and as one with the consciousness of the Maha Chohan, the Great Lord, who is the representative of the Holy Spirit to earth's evolutions. Thus, by our coming and by our nearness each of you may call for your divine awakening in the Presence of God.

Be ready, for the dawn of your resurrection will come! And one day, when your earthly mission is through, there will come to you, stirring through you like the wind in the pines, the ascension currents that will accelerate your soul and inner being, raising you to eternal oneness with your God Presence. Only then will you experience the fullness of the benediction "For thine is the Kingdom, and the Power, and the Glory forever."

Please meditate, dear ones, on these words. That you might enter in to my Cosmic Christ Consciousness and the full momentum of my Causal Body, so that I may assist you to rise into your own God estate, is my prayer.

I bless you, I love you, and I adorn you with celestial flowers.

The Cosmic Christ
Lord Maitreya

Beloved children of my heart—my endearing young charms that I gaze on so fondly today—can I add to his words? I humbly bow to him . . . Until we meet, keep on in your Light meditation for yourselves and the Light-bearers of the world. Truly we move mountains!

Eternal blessings,

El Morya

P.S. We will unite in satsanga* with the Brotherhood with our opening meditation May 28 at 11:00 a.m. MST, concluding with our full rituals beginning at 9:00 p.m. MST.

April 7, 1957

---

*satsanga [Sanskrit, sat: "good, true," sanga: "company"]: fellowship with truth; communion with holy people, as in a spiritual gathering; company or meeting of spiritual seekers.

26

Ashram Notes

As the engulfing fog wraps a city, so the ooze of human emotions smothers hearts, cutting off the frail identity from the compassionate Christ. Not the least of these enshrouding emotions is spiritual pride.

For the benefit of those entering the Path as well as those who are students of many years, I say the stumbling block of spiritual pride must be squarely faced. Spiritual pride is a blinding force, so much so that those who are coated with it do not see it or its dangers.

Spiritual pride gives those who possess it a certain sense of superiority in their pursuit of spiritual goals, allowing them to remain aloof from the coarser vibrations of a materialistic life-style. The exclusivity of being among the "enlightened" and above the "ignorant masses" effectively separates such people from the true path of being their brother's keeper and from fellowship with God and the ascended and unascended brethren—as surely as walls of steel separate your bodies of flesh from one another.

It is just as easy for the adept as it is for the neophyte to lose sight of the goals of eternity. Once one takes the plunge into a sea of indifference in the private self-centered pursuit of the mysteries of the kingdom, he is too desensitized and sanitized to be aware of the needs of others. In the process of dehumanizing the path, both adept and neophyte may discount all the comfort and the assistance that God has afforded them in their seeking and finding the Truth through the avenues opened by the Ascended Masters.

Consider the imperishable power of Love! The gospel of God that the apostle Paul wrote to the Christians in Rome was an imperishable message, which we would do well to remember today:

> Who shall separate us from the love of Christ? shall tribulation, or distress, or persecution, or famine, or nakedness, or peril, or sword?
>
> As it is written, For thy sake we are killed all the day long; we are accounted as sheep for the slaughter.
>
> Nay, in all these things we are more than conquerors through him that loved us.
>
> For I am persuaded, that neither death, nor life, nor [fallen] angels, nor [their] principalities, nor [their] powers, nor things present, nor things to come,
>
> Nor height, nor depth, nor any other creature, shall be able to separate us from the love of God, which is in Christ Jesus our Lord.

Above all, let chelas of the will of God not allow spiritual pride to separate them from the love of Christ in one another, betwixt Christ and his Mystical Body on earth and in heaven, or between themselves and Hierarchy, who stands to initiate them by Christ's love.

The magnet of Love draws us to God. "We love him," as beloved Jesus said, "because he first loved us." The Master pointed out the deceit and the conceit of pretending to love God while hating one's brother: "If a man say, I love God, and hateth his brother, he is a liar: for he that loveth not his brother whom he hath seen, how can he love God whom he hath not seen?" Whereupon he gave us the commandment that "he who loveth God love his brother also."

Human rationalizations and denials of the out-of-alignment state menace the real peace of your soul and stop all progress on the Path. For to be lulled into a false sense of security while not living in Christ-Truth but living in the lie of the synthetic self is pitiful and patently unreal.

May the dissolving rays born in the heart-flame of God himself pour through your disturbed and disturbing emotions. As shafts of purity, these rays dart forth from your I AM Presence to draw you to the shining pathway of the divine experience.

Here you lose sight of pride's pettiness and utter selfishness as you behold the beauty of the Infinite One, who simply *is* your Real Self complete. Face to face with the glory of God, you no longer have need of the defense mechanisms of spiritual, intellectual or human pride.

You cannot, you dare not let anything—especially pride in any of its forms—separate you from the Love of Christ-Truth!

Very early on the Path pride may be piqued when the Master gives correction to the chela.

Unwillingness to take correction or to admit that one needs correction has terminated the path for many a potential chela. Therefore, you must not forget Jesus' teaching recorded in the Book of Hebrews:

"My son, despise not thou the chastening of the Lord [i.e., the Guru], nor faint when thou art rebuked of him: For whom the Lord loveth he chasteneth, and scourgeth every son whom he receiveth. If ye endure chastening, God dealeth with you as with sons; for what son is he whom the father chasteneth not?"

It is also written that the administration of the law of karma belongs solely to God and the spiritual overseers whom he appoints; therefore take care that in your pride you do not take the law into your own hands. For the LORD has said:

"To me belongeth vengeance, and recompense; their foot shall slide in due time: for the day of their calamity [karma] is at hand, and the things that shall come upon them make haste. . . . Vengeance is mine; I will repay."

I am sending you my ray, whose vibration will help you to understand the expression of God (i.e., God's expressing of himself) through the many. You who are working on this ray of God's will by the decree of your good karma may in divine justice forge imperishable links of the Spirit both here below and in the octaves of Light.

Above all, have an untainted Love. For untainted Love is the panacea of eternity for spiritual pride and separateness. Love gives of itself to supply every need of the children of the Father-Mother God. Only Love allows one to see one's pride and to put it aside for the taking up of the garment of honor and humility.

Work in the world as the Lord's hands and feet. Be not weary in well doing, for not alone in Darjeeling shall you who hold to the will of God be honored guests but in the pulsating heart-center of the God-head itself.

Again, I bid you adieu. Seek God like the hound of heaven but succor one another with the milk of divine kindness. Love and let love, lest you lose the balance of your Christ flame and the perspective of what is real and what is not about yourself.

I seal you—all of my children—in goodwill.

Eternal blessings,

27

Ashram Notes

Our arms are always outstretched, reaching for the chelas who persistently widen the gap between themselves and the Ascended Masters. They imagine us to be far from them, and so we are—for thinking makes it so. Let us think: time is not, space is not. The borders of the Shekinah glory cannot be told from its center. All is One. Let us erase artificial distances and embrace across the miles.

Arms succor each wound, heal and bless you— yes, yes. But our heritage sublime slips from view with the passing of Daylight and the approach of Nightfall. In Darkness many lose the vision of their soul beauty. Like the stripes of a lash, such loss should make you leap toward the Light.

How beautiful, how precious the simple thought— beauty. As flowers are God's fleeting thoughts imperfectly communicated to man because of his faded faculties of discernment, so the thought about beauty has escaped him for want of the chalice of the mind upraised.

You think to attain increased consciousness of the Spirit. You seek a fantastic formula, a miraculous remedy, as it were. Yet the thought about beauty is ignored! Beauty as the cure, mind you.

One needs a kindred spirit for association. Yet if the thought of ugliness is retained to taint the soul, how shall the Father feel the kindred sense with that which to him is bastard?

In preparing you for the Ashram, I advocate not as one who has not tasted the test but as one who has viewed both the ugly and the beautiful.

The rumblings of old errors may sway the branches; they will never sever the root. Only by thy God shalt thou make this calling sure. By the sense of beauty one shall cognize Christ. The waters of affliction smitten by the rod of initiation shall part, and the soul shall pass over a sea of errors to the Promised Land.

Shall one seek arhatship* for escape into bliss or shall one attain as a co-laborer with God? Who is enlightened and shall cry, "Nirvana!" The Spirit of the LORD would lift up the downtrodden, heal the afflicted and bless the broken-hearted.

O labor, chosen ones, for the Holy One has called thee. How can you sleep when our Ashram call has gone forth? The cries of the children of God are about healing, about wisdom, about salvation. Send forth the thought. Many laborers in the vineyard need the solace of our sending. At the appointed times be in that Spirit.

Who is worthy?

Who is on the LORD's side?

Who has a greater love?

Be lifted.

Remember Magdalene, and sin cannot hold thee back.

Be caught up in the sacred chariot of fire.

*The Buddhist term *arhat* (Sanskrit, "worthy one") refers to a saint who has perfected himself, overcome all obstacles to enlightenment and attained the goal of nirvana. *Arhatship* refers to the state or process of embodying the qualities and nature of an *arhat*; or the life of maintaining oneself as an *arhat*.

Remember Elijah, and thy atoms of flesh cannot hold thee back.

Stand in the secret place of the Most High.

Remember Enoch, and thine own ego shall not hold thee back.

A fire breaks forth upon the mountain. The cup of joy trembleth for you, children of Zion seeking your perfection. This ye seek, better to serve! The answer lies in beauty. Morya has placed his heart before Christ, saying, "Make this thy garden."

O my God, for thy cause and with thy benediction through Saint Germain, I ask that all recipients of our Ashram Notes who sincerely strive to assimilate thy Word and to activate thy Work be given a transmittal of our Power, our Wisdom and our Love. That my Ashram for thee be established, visible once again to the eyes of men, is my fondest hope.

My America, may the wisdom of the East be brought to beauty's perfection in thee. May the knowledge of freedom and of our God cover the earth. As the Lord has put his blessed hand upon us, so may we also go to the lost sheep of the house of Israel, saying, "The kingdom of heaven is at hand!"

In his name let us "heal the sick, cleanse the lepers, raise the dead, cast out demons" and work a marvelous work for the faith! Freely have we received, freely may we give.

Rejoice together in labor now. Labor henceforth for beauty; make it perpetual. Remember, God shall reward you openly for your secret labor.

Morya El

28

Ashram Notes

A dry cistern needs rain—so shall every one who is empty be filled when the latter rain falls. The omnipresence of the Holy Spirit passes unrecognized among men who are pressed hard by their own delusions.

Saint Peter well said, "Gird up the loins of your mind, be sober, and hope to the end for the grace that is to be brought unto you at the revelation of Jesus Christ. . . . Because it is written: Be ye holy, for I am holy."

We must never underestimate the pull and the subtle influences exerted upon us by others' thoughts. For our reaction to the negative can be colossal. Yet, consider the benign influences. Let us heed them.

That is why the LORD of hosts has said, "Not by might, nor by power, but by my Spirit." Cast your anchor into the sanctuary. For though the pull may create drift, one can always draw on the rope and thereby return through the veil to the holy place.

Many are the cupidities of the gray ones. Their masks are full of beauty and their words abound with axiomatic truth. But error is sheathed in its scabbard, hidden in their cloaks, awaiting the moment to strike.

The servants and the sons should equally beware. The measuring stick of peculiar and real value is truly the flame of the Holy Ghost.

Remember that God does not impute unrighteousness unto himself. Be thou yoked therefore to the anchor of the Spirit. And see to it that unrighteousness be not imputed to thee.

The cries of the fearful rise up to the Mother of the World, but those whose cries are heeded most are sons able to bear burdens. The Mother has daughters like unto herself, able to offer consolation and strength through purity of heart.

In these days know the strength of the old schools of Light, who guarded the flame of the Ancient of Days. Know that you have believed in the One who has been from the foundation of the world. Though dying oft, he lives again today. His vibration comes to us wavelike, full of power, full of the Holy Ghost, with holy healing in his wings.

I AM the Resurrection and the Life. Say it!

29

Ashram Notes

Opportunity blossoms seedlike, silently in the heart of the earth; the rich soil quietly conceals the sown germs of Light gestating for a purpose.

The Sower went forth to sow the word of God. You must not rely upon seeds scattered among thorns, for these are choked by the wild growth of false beginnings and the snares of the tempter. Nor should you rely upon seeds fallen by the wayside, for these are devoured by the fowls of Satan sent to take away the word sown in the hearts of Christ's little ones.

Cultivate your garden with care; prepare the good ground for the seed that yields the fruit of the word. Begin the first steps even now. Plow your plot.

Communion with elemental beings of Nature, with sons of Light and with angels can be profitable. These three doors lead Godward.

How shall he who cannot work with the seeds of God implanted in the footstool kingdom cognize the pure seeds of Light descended to create beauty, harmony and joy?

One need not destroy when one can transmute. One need not tear down the old foundations when the permutation of molecules by the violet ray can make them new.

The cry of Babylon is great in these days. Let us rise up and go down to the cities of the earth and revive Love, which though dead in some is ever new in our hearts.

Blessed be ye who hear and most blessed be ye who do. The Ashram still shines dimly this year. Shall the coming days see a greater flowering?

30

Ashram Notes

Is a thought needed? Ur shall supply it.

Noble aspirations we laud. The longing for knowledge of the Spirit is commendable. Such longing is satisfied only by true spiritual growth and by the magnitude of the spirit.

Cultivate patience. This is needed, else the spiral is but loosely knit and the whole structure unable to bear the pressures of cosmos.

Better a small but well-built stable than a glorious mansion where the wind of variance passes through the chinks. The ordinary eye may not reveal the leakage, but the eye of the arhat needs not a second glance.

"In your patience possess ye your souls" was the Master's counsel. "For ye have need of patience," his disciple explained, "that, after ye have done the will of God, ye might receive the promise. For yet a little while, and he that shall come will come, and will not tarry."

While there is yet time, seek the magnitude of the spirit. You will be more precious, for you are precious to me now.

Consider the balm of achievement, of foundations well laid, of the fruit of striving. Ponder, too, the fragrance of your lives as sendings to the Mother of the World. With such incense do we adorn heaven's altar.

Know you not that you are the heirs of the Most High? And the joint-heirs of the kingdom?

Let your thoughts continually attune with Christ. The flame within may suddenly kindle the whole bush. The dry branches with the green will rejoice in the consecration of wholeness.

The weight of karma must be laid aside. On wings of light the spirit must strive for the Divine Union. Here is no imputation. Here is righteousness.

Seek the right use of life's hours. Though eternity be your chalice, waste not a drop of the costly substance of time. I do not say you shall not rest, but let the rest be as the pause between heartbeats, that the next thrust may propel you to more meaningful goals. Thus attained Hercules; thus were the Augean stables cleansed.

Life woven of light and sound is harmonious, especially if a penetration of one's spirit ensue. Such co-measurement of the outer life with the inner establishes the law of harmony even in your atoms of flesh.

Are there many spirits or many manifestations of the One? The Elders of Light are one. They that press in to the inner circle become one. Only without is separation. The elder seeks but to serve the younger. Youth receives the wisdom of age and in turn gives her strength; thus shall the structure rise.

Morya stands in devotion and service to the Mother of the World. Of old her devotees were blessed,

for the womb of the Mother has succored many avatars. Many arhats have sprung forth thence.

The life of service to the Brotherhood exceeds
all personality, which, if it is to have a life of its own,
must change from error to Truth, from gold to the
refined spirit. But then it will no longer be the
personality, for it will have become the impersonal
personality of Christ. And the leftover straws of the
human personality shall pass away with the coming
consummation of the holy breath of the Flame.

My abode is the whirlwind. Seek me not, then,
in the lowlands of the lesser personality. Yet do I love
you personally each one!

My blessing be to you,

31

Ashram Notes

Early this morning, as the dawn poured out her first ray from the roseate chalice of God's love, I stood in the doorway of our Darjeeling Ashram to greet you through time and space with a living salutation from the higher octaves of Light.

Child of Light, friends of old, and newly found friends, I would sing you a song from my heart's musings written a century ago:*

No, the heart that has truly loved never forgets,
But as truly loves on to the close,
As the sunflower turns on her god when he sets
The same look which she turned when he rose!

Because I loved you then and I love you still, you are welcome here as God's child and I shall never think of you in any other way.

I sincerely hope that you will come to know the meaning, as well as the blessing, of "holding the immaculate concept" on behalf of any and all of God's children. The assistance you give and the

---

*El Morya was embodied as Thomas Moore (1779–1852), poet laureate of Ireland. "Believe Me, If All Those Endearing Young Charms," excerpted here, is one of his best-loved poems. Other favorites include: "The Harp That Once through Tara's Halls," "The Loves of the Angels," and "Lalla Rookh."

assistance you receive when you behold the immaculate pattern of God-given perfection for another is a thing of beauty and a divine joy forever.

We have decreed that the Ashram be dedicated to the will of God. And we have prepared a place where the mind can dwell in the wisdom of his presence. This we call the Ashramic consciousness. Here our love, yours and mine, of doing the will of God permeates the atmosphere! For from the Creation the flame of that will has been dispersed in seed form into every heart, into every cell, into every atom.

This seed of Light you also received through proximity to your mother's heart flame when you were yet in the womb. And she likewise received it through her progenitors, who go back to the point of origin in the Word where God fashioned the heart of the first Mother of the World.

And so today within your heart's chalice there blazes a tiny flame of God's own will from his own heart. To teach you how to fan it to a diamond brilliance, how to expand its Light, is our gift to you who are the builders of the Ashram.

I AM invoking the Light of God that never fails, to pierce the clouds of maya and break through the atomic, gross world of form to consume its sorrows and pain where these have burdened your heart.

I AM invoking the Light of God that never fails, to direct into your lifestream the vibrations of healing harmony amplified by the angels of the Maha Chohan.

I AM pouring upon your head the oil of peace from the heart of the Elohim of Peace. And I touch your chakras with this holy oil to restore the balance of cycles.

Peace be still. Peace be unto you.

Allow yourself to be drawn close to our orbit in the coming days, for we shall initiate through your soul chakra a victorious momentum that can turn the wilderness of the human consciousness into that lovely Eden, where conversation with God is an hourly possibility. This will take place individual by individual in those who will accept and guard the gift.

Whether your present rate of progress be maintained on the high road or the low, so long as you are steady and steadfast in your gait, I shall continue to pray for you as I do, that you become wider and deeper channels for the pure love of God as you do your part to help bring in God's kingdom of beauty and love on earth.

Unite hearts! Never, never divide. May you be an instrument in your Mother's hands, even as you are in your Father's. Through your service and love may the whole wide, wide world be blessed. We of the Ashram salute you, O child of the Divine!

I AM victorious in the Light
and I bless you eternally,

Morya El

32

Ashram Notes

The chelas of my Ashram are like Joseph's coat of many colors. Although they are varied in personality, we the Ascended Masters weave them together as one in a truly seamless garment. Such is the immaculate concept we hold for the devotees who day by day are becoming the true spirit of our Ashram.

We use the sacred fire of God to charge your individual worlds with the conception of beauty as we know it on the etheric and causal levels. We step down its vibration so that you can behold it. Its powerful thoughtform acts as a unifying factor in your world as you creatively multiply it by your threefold flame, fusing hearts in a divine oneness, thus forming an Ashramic consciousness in the highest sense.

Faithfully practice the rituals, knowing that your calls will help to relieve pressures having to do with planetary conditions that are borne by the Ascended Masters and the unascended initiates who study with us.

When you, too, take on as part of your Ashram work some small percentage of the weight of world karma, you will see the fruit of your effort manifesting all around you. Moreover, your world service will help to balance some of your personal karma, freeing you to do the will of God, as your heart desires. And thereby you may reap in this day the bounties of God's perfection that you have called forth.

When I train new students, my object is to teach them how to weave strands of Light-substance from their individual worlds to ours. Thus we attempt to bridge the chasm of consciousness—that great gulf between the finite and the infinite, across which no human mind can pass of its own effort.

Through attunement with us in your daily use of the rituals, you will find the strands of Light-substance becoming more substantial until, like diamond cables of indestructibility, our linkages become a safe highway over which your soul may freely travel at will.

Be alert to discern the subtle differences between freedom and bondage. The razor's edge of discrimination must be walked by the disciple who cherishes his new-found freedom as a spiritual heritage from the Great White Brotherhood.

Freedom is not to walk destructively and later be subject to the bondage of a destructive karma rebounded. If you need a reminder, bind on your heart the law of doing God's will so that freedom may indeed be your future prize.

Those chelas who will with confidence put their hand securely in mine, knowing the unity of their own Holy Christ Selves with the Elder Brothers, will never regret this step as long as it be sincerely taken.

Remember, every hand extended upward to us is a receiving one. To balance the matter, the chela's giving hand must reach out through the Darkness to perform acts in my name.

I watch from the Ashram turret as you grow in love, and in service to the Light that shines even through the severest storm.

Eternal blessings,

33

Ashram Notes

With joy I bring you the words of the beloved Ascended Master Saint Germain.

Out of sheer despair I at times in my past embodiments forged great sustaining links with the Brotherhood. And out of his merciful heart God endowed me with an everlasting strength and a hope for a brighter tomorrow.

You who tread the Path today, who are facing situations much like those I had to deal with, would do well to bear up under the pressures of your dire moods and determine not to give in to them, even when it seems you are unable to change them.

The key to remaining anchored in the Light through the thick and thin of the ups and downs of mood swings is to follow a regimen of ordered service to God and the heavenly host.

Just as some of you have set up your altars in a room set aside where you regularly commune with your God, so you can establish cooperation with the Great White Brotherhood as a ritual in your heart.

This daily service will indeed see you through many a dire mood, even despondency.

Ordering your life in a cooperative venture with the Ascended Masters, such as building our world-wide Ashram as a source of support to millions, will lift your spirits to a pinnacle of hope through the vision you will gain in the strength of our oneness.

Lifted up to the Mount of Transfiguration day by day through ordered service, you will see a magnificent panorama of the God-design for our beloved planet, a player among other planetary players in a majestically ordered cosmos whose spheres move in their ritualed courses, keeping the cadences of time and eternity as coordinates of a cosmic clock. We visualize this perpetual motion machine we call our cosmos resting as a jewel in the heart of God.

Dearly endowed hearts, call to me and I *will* answer! I AM here to help you as you help yourself through Christ, who is the bastion of our joint effort, to free a planet from every vestige of sin and its attendant sorrow until God in action in you shall wipe away all tears from the eyes of his people.

For it is written that "there shall be no more death, neither sorrow, nor crying, neither shall there be any more pain: for the former things are passed away" that have prevented his children from manifesting the perfection which is suspended so gloriously above them in their Electronic God Presence, awaiting externalization both here and now.

May you be divine mothers all and deliverers in Christ's name, attending the reunion of the soul with her true God Self. Even so, clear the way for the angels who shall deliver God's people in your name.

May the blue canopy of our Ashram cover the world; for, lo, the Mother of the World cometh at midnight, and at noon.

I AM lovingly yours,
Saint Germain

Blessings,

34

Ashram Notes

Having just returned to the planet from "parts unknown" to be with you during this holiday season, I pen this Ashram Note for the upliftment of your spirits. This remark may seem strange at first, but if you stop and think about it, my travels are no more strange than your own journeyings to and fro upon the earth.

For inasmuch as our estate is one of complete freedom in God, we are at home anywhere in the universe and come and go with ease. May you one day know this freedom in God to travel in a universe you also call Home.

I write herewith my message especially for the children of the Diamond Heart. Remember, it is your responsibility to harness the energies of your individual worlds. This is important. Unbridled forces of desire create many conflicts; and suffering is become rampant through the ceaseless hammerings of the "Gimme! Gimme!" of the human ego.

Silently the precious Spirit of God hovers over the earth, observing the extension of its own life-force to several billion beating hearts. As one watches this beautiful display of the Light rays from God's heart flashing forth into humanity's realm, one finds it hard to comprehend that there could be any other manifestation except God's limitless Light and Love.

That the wayward children of earth may soon learn to share God's eternal goodwill in peace is our fervent hope. But if they are to learn, who will teach them? Can they change their ways without mentors who will show them good reason why they should? They seek benefits; therefore, my chelas, reveal to them the benefits to be derived from serving the Light so freely given rather than just using it to gain short-sighted goals.

Tonight we are gently showering upon you our blessings from the higher planes. Like snowflakes they settle upon you in commemoration of the nativity of Jesus of Nazareth. These "snowflakes" are actually miniature electronic crystals charged with Light's transparent purity, perfection and joy.

In some, an iridescent blue flame dances in a sapphire of God's will, forming a fiery nucleus of the blue Buddha. In others, maltese crosses of amethyst crystal provide the chalice for violet/purple/pink flames that pulsate in honor of Saint Germain.

These snowflake thoughtforms are conceived in the hearts of the Ascended Masters, and they carry a clarion recording of the Masters' vibrations. Be receptive to these momentums of Good from the Masters' Christ nature by opening your heart to them.

Then simply let the warmth of your God Flame cause the snowflakes to melt and blend their contents with your own being. For they will add a radiant expansion of your divine nature to the focus of God's Light within you. Being so blessed, you will naturally enter in to that rejoicing which may truly be called the Christmas Spirit.

Receive this crystallized dew of heaven as nourishment for your spiritual nature even as the children of Israel received the manna in the wilderness for their physical sustenance.

Do not misqualify these molecules by bringing them down to the level of human conflict. Do not rob these charged particles of their life merely to sustain your human will or whim.

Now say, "I decree and I accept that the ascended host's Christmas gift to me of these snowflakes will crystallize gifts of gold, frankincense and myrrh within my purest spiritual nature."

O children of the Diamond Heart, seize these treasures as they come tumbling into your world!

Find the point of equipoise in the heart of the Christ Child from which you can commend your soul into your Father's hands. For here in the Infant Divine is Life—eternal and victorious—yours to claim.

I tell you, becoming a Christ is both the easiest and the hardest thing you will ever do, depending on your perspective. This change from the human to the divine nature is wrought in spirit and not without a struggle. For by cosmic law the human must be changed into the divine nature ere it pass through the veil to realms of Light.

Christ was forty days and nights in the wilderness, yet in all the temptations of Satan he overcame.

Consider, too, how Jacob wrestled with the angel through the night unto the breaking of the day. And he would not let the angel go until he would bless him. For Jacob knew the blessing would be for his transformation by the Spirit of the LORD from the human to the divine.

Because of Jacob's valor in the struggle against the not-self, the angel pronounced that Jacob would henceforth be called Israel (which translates from the Hebrew, "He will rule as God"). For, he said, "as a prince hast thou power with God and with man and hast prevailed."

And the angel blessed him, i.e., initiated him. And Jacob called the place Peniel: "For I have seen God face to face and my life is preserved."

A clue to the necessity for the initiate to "fulfill all righteousness" and "suffer all things" was given when Jesus said concerning John the Baptist, "Among them that are born of women there hath not risen a greater than John the Baptist: notwithstanding he that is least in the kingdom of heaven is greater than he."

This means that all of the issue of God who enter the human frame and framework must fulfill the right use of the Law and suffer their share of planetary karma. For here on earth they are prisoners of "the lowly estate of the flesh." And here they must break its bonds through the Guru-chela relationship on a path of personal Christhood, whereas the least in the kingdom of heaven are beyond the confines of the flesh, hence in greater glory.

Through this Ashram work, you the chela and I the Guru will gradually become better acquainted; and it is this tie that will be of real assistance to you. I tell you sincerely that friendship with an ascended being is invaluable while you are balancing your karma, attaining your victory over Death and Hell, and winning your ascension unto the life everlasting.

Perhaps I try your patience by not writing to you as often as you would like me to, but (and forgive me for saying this) some of you have never written to me! Maybe you are afraid of me and think of me as a gruff old man, as someone once referred to me.

Ah, dear hearts, such is not the case. Fear not, for if you ever come to Darjeeling, you will see how warmly I welcome you. And you will know my heart's love for my chelas as expressed in these words I wrote as Thomas Moore:

> Ask not if still I love,
>   Too plain these eyes have told thee;
> Too well their tears must prove
>   How near and dear I hold thee. . . .
>
> 'T is not in pleasure's idle hour
>   That thou canst know affection's power.
> No, try its strength in grief or pain;
>   Attempt as now its bonds to sever,
> Thou'lt find true love's a chain
>   That binds for ever!*

Please know that cosmic law directs and controls all things, including my letters to you. Thus I write these letters through my amanuensis as the Great Law allows, and they are forwarded to you by my trusted chelas in our Ashram.

Many assignments occupy my time and space, for I am here and I am there, sometimes in Darjeeling or in Egypt, then in Washington, and again away on cosmic business.

We must all be about our Father's business. Graduation from earth's schoolrooms, as I have so

*Thomas Moore, "Ask Not If Still I Love."

well found out, is but a further opportunity in this solar system and beyond for wider service to our "little brothers," as dear Kuthumi calls them.

Lift up your eyes toward the heavens above, where dwells that loving presence—the Great Silent Watcher—and relax your grip on earthly things. Try to forsake (at least temporarily) your day-to-day concerns.

Dear hearts, if you could but see the graceful angelic beings who are simply pulsing with Divine Love, and longing to reach into your worlds to assist you in drinking in the beauties and joys of this season so filled with the essences of Christ's Love (which are borne between hearts like floating lotus blossoms on a clear pond)—if you could but see the radiant pink, blue and gold auras of these angelic beings as they send their blessing into your world, I am certain the sight of them would lift you up almost into the very air.

I am counting on you to sustain on earth in the coming new year the angelic gifts of Love we have transmitted to you in these blessed snowflakes. And may you happily share the joy of the angelic hosts in the greatest gift of all:

> For God so loved the world, that he gave his only begotten Son, that whosoever believeth in him should not perish, but have everlasting life.

Victory is ours through the Son of God.

Eternal Christmas blessings,

Morya El

35

Ashram Notes

Beloved Children of Goodwill,

Wise is the soul who can with ease relinquish habits that have bound her. The Path grows easier as flowers of the Spirit are strewn by happy elementals beneath the feet of the pilgrim.

Some will ask: What are these flowers? We answer: Is not kindness to another in word and deed an immortelle according to the law of karma?

Others will ask: Is all karma evil, or do the Lords of Karma record also the benign? My children, Morya smiles.

What of the power of radiation? The Solar Lords provide extraordinary rays of physical light to all living things. The chlorophyll in plants traps the energy of sunlight and, with the help of carbon dioxide and water, converts it to the energy of glucose. Thus the alchemy within the green chlorophyll has the ability to nourish all life.

Who, then, will provide the spiritual radiation of the Light of the Son of God for the "huddled masses yearning to breathe free" from their self-imposed states of bondage?

It can be agreed that God, like the Great Central Sun, ever radiates his attributes, which are all benign, upon the just and the unjust. Yes? Yes—and so the heart pump also beats from the sun center of the body temple. But without the chemism of certain cells that transport the oxygen from the heart through the blood to the body cells, the whole organism would perish.

And so we learn about the law of the universal interdependence of all life. And so chelas become microcosmic sun-centers of Christ's radiance, vital to the life of lesser manifestations who look to them as their solar source. Where my chelas are, let the Son of God be the deliverer of men and nations!

Who among you can uphold a city, a nation, yea, even a planet? Do not be surprised if you may be asked to try. And if you try, be forewarned that you will succeed *only* through the balanced, developed, masterful threefold flame of Christ within your heart. Thus fan Love, fan Wisdom, and lastly fan Power. Many may succeed by God's grace, multiplying their own good works through an established Christhood.

The Lord's inheritance held in trust for the joint-heirs of Christ is unlimited and grand. But only those who can contain it can claim it. Therefore strengthen the vessel of the heart that it might contain Christ's treasures.

My disciples must not limit their opportunities for practical spiritual growth. We have graduated many fine souls from life's schoolrooms; some from planet earth who received their degrees cum laude and with other high honors are serving the sheep of the Good Shepherd in cosmic pastures.

Disciples are needed for cosmic work; these must prepare themselves not only to bear the weight of the Shepherd's mantle but also to wield it in defense of the sheep. Therefore, let the worthy ready themselves for the Call of the Most High for true shepherds when it shall go forth unto the borders of his kingdom.

As you strive for perfection and aspire to Love, the Ashram spiral is built.

Why do I repeat so often, "Call to our octave for the healing of the world"? Is it not because I should embolden you to fill His magnanimity with Light? Be bold. Begin most generously to dispense my love, which I transfer to you as a healing oil from the pine forests at the feet of the mountain.

Like the aromatic resin of balsam, called the balm of Gilead, the helping, healing oil of God's will transferred through your hands will comfort the Lord's other sheep which are not of this fold. Them we must also bring, that they, too, might hear Christ's voice.

Remember Saint Thérèse, who determined to be a master craftsman of intercession for others and succeeded. Like a rose of heaven, she remains close to the heart of God. Can you not be rosebuds, spreading your gentle perfume to souls languishing on earth today who so sorely need it? I think so.

Eternal blessings,

Morya El

We thank you for your sweet letters and love gifts, without which this work could not continue on the physical plane. The Master conveys his Light, Energy and Consciousness to you; his words are cups on a conveyer belt. As you read and reread, study and meditate upon these Notes, the cups empty themselves of his offering as they travel on track through your mind.

Freely ye receive, freely give. This is the law of your Christhood. Therefore be reminded of your obligation to all life to multiply by your expanding threefold flame the blessings received and to send them on their way to God's children who look to you as the nexus of Hierarchy in their worlds.

Thus fulfill the law of Alpha and Omega. Thus maintain the balance of forces in your Being. Thus self-empty that you might be refilled by the Great God Self, who delivers to you your portion through the blessed Guru Morya El.

I AM blessing you always in the Light of God that never fails.

Mark

February 27, 1958

36

Ashram Notes

Beloved Children of the Light,

Jewels are esteemed, but who has recognized the precious stones, lodestones I should say, that God has placed within a living soul? Passports to eternal Life we call them.

Remember to be attentive to your rates of vibration. Beware lest they fall dangerously low or rise dangerously high. How so?

The low vibration invites intruders from lower astral planes who creep into your psyche unawares, blending in with the environment you have created by your vibratory rate. The high vibration invites attackers who are also from the lower astral planes. These aggressively attack the citadel of the psyche, scaling the walls to take you *and* your Light by surprise or subterfuge. Take care, for both the passive and the active entities be cunning.

Therefore measure your rates of vibration. Strive for balance at the level of your Holy Christ Self and thereby invoke the maximum protection of the Great Law, which is given to those who keep the flame of the Christ consciousness on earth.

Know, then, that Ur says the spirits of imperiling irritation or imperious anger would be quickly driven out of the house by every disciple if the dampening effect they have on the physical heart and the heart chakra were known or the murky colorations they turn the aura could be seen. And so it is with other spirits of darkness that emerge from levels of human or sub-human origin.

Conversely, when people begin to see outpictured on their physical bodies and chakras as well as on their spiritual garments the beneficial effects of vibrations of beauty and love as well as the constructive forces of their inner divinity, they will flock to the cosmic marts seeking this adornment in place of cosmetics and synthetics, which only cover over the negative outcroppings of their negative vibrations.

You are familiar with Jesus' saying about the Pharisees being the "blind leaders of the blind," that if the blind lead the blind, both shall fall into the ditch. Well, we counsel you to have compassion on the blind as Jesus did and to heal them in his name.

Thus emulate the Christ, who said of the man born blind that he was born blind so that "the works of God should be made manifest in him." May you also use your infirmities to glorify God and as an opportunity to atone for personal and planetary karma.

At the conclusion of your ritual meditations and mantrams, direct the healing Light to those who ask you to pray for them in their afflictions. Visualize a shaft of white light tinged with the emerald color of heaven's healing green descending from your I AM Presence, passing through the heart of your Christ Self and then being released through your own heart

chakra to the one whose suffering you would allevi-
ate. Be sure to see this shaft of Light as an all-
powerful beacon of intense whiteness. See it enter the
body of the afflicted one through and under the
direction of his Holy Christ Self.

This is important. For the Holy Christ Self is
the Mediator of the Light and the true personal
physician of each one. The Holy Christ Self will
prescribe and regulate the quality and quantity of
Light that can be absorbed and applied to all of one's
needs and not just a particular condition. For the
Holy Christ Self deals in wholeness and the healing of
the whole manifestation from the inner to the outer,
from cause to effect.

Observe the quality of your heart, both spiritually and physically. Ask Jesus to purge and purify
your heart of all hardness of heart, non-mercy and
non-forgiveness—of all impure desire and possessive
love. Ask Jesus to show you what you need to do to
make your heart a chalice of Christ's Love and an
instrument of his Sacred Heart. Ask Jesus to receive
your heart and fashion it anew, acceptable unto the
LORD, your beloved I AM Presence.

When you have done this, apply to the Lord
through the inner corona, and he will reveal to you
the mysteries of the kingdom and the hidden things
of God; he will even quicken in you the living
remembrance of the Christ, saying two thousand
years ago and today, "Feed my sheep." And your soul
shall both hear and see the Lord, and *you will feed
his sheep!*

People must awaken from the nightmare of
Armageddon to the surrounding kingdom of the Lord

of Life as a living reality. Be prepared for any eventuality in the physical octave so that you be not swept away by karmic circumstances seemingly beyond your control, for the jeweled treasure within you is a priceless gift of God. It will not fail you if you do not fail it.

Esteem most highly the things of the Spirit. Meditate upon the Word and the Law of God. Know the kingdom of the Over-Soul in peace, peace, peace, and the peace-commanding Presence of the Christ. Surely where your treasure is, there will your heart be also.

If it be the will of God that the blind be made whole, then your prayers for healing shall be answered; if not, as is often the case, then teach that one how to first heal himself of a spiritual blindness that blinds him to the karmic causes from past lives that have resulted in his blindness in this life.

Teach him that if his soul be healed and he diligently balance his karma by selfless service and the violet flame, then he shall attain the kingdom. If he seek healing for the body, he may receive it; but he may not attain the kingdom.

The heart of Morya is a diamond castle that rises on the hillside of the world where the morning and the evening star casts its beam. The castle gates are open to those who, in the spirit of divine confidence in the Father, can say without reserve, "Thy will be done!"

Let them enter my Diamond Heart who fear not to pursue the path of truest Love, seeking, as Kuthumi has stressed, never to divide but always to unite hearts of goodwill.

Children, my blue ray directs to you all the blessings of the angels of the fiery blue diamond of God's will. These angels carry his bounty of goodness into your world, renewed moment by moment, that you may know what I mean when I say,

Eternal blessings,

El Morya

37

Ashram Notes

My Beloved Disciples,

In his letter to the Galatians Paul wrote: "Bear ye one another's burdens and so fulfill the law of Christ." Yet three verses later we read, "Every man shall bear his own burden."

While I cite the apparent contradiction in these two passages of scripture, I would underscore that the harmony of the full circle of the law reveals the consistency of these two statements within their context.

First, know that the "burden" referred to is the burden of one's karma. Then know that although the law of karma decrees that every man must bear his own karmic burden, the law of grace through Jesus Christ mitigates this law of Moses, which comes down to us from the Old Testament.

Through the grace of the Christ flame in your heart and through your oneness with Christ Jesus, the burden-bearer of the Piscean age, you may intercede for a brother or sister to bear that one's burden in time of great need by asking God to allow you to carry that portion of another's karma which it is lawful for you to carry. To take on another's karma when you see that one falling beneath the weight of his karmic cross does indeed fulfill the law of Christ.

There are times, however, when it is the better part of valor, as Christ's discretion would have it, to leave well enough alone and let your neighbor bear his karmic burden, for only thus shall he learn the lessons his karma is sent to teach him. Nevertheless, Christly compassion and divine helpfulness are always in order when your neighbor is struggling through the trials and tribulations of his karma.

But know that it is written in the Law that the karma that is borne for another (as the strong uphold the weak), whether it be by the blessed Saviour or by your Christ Self working with you and through you, must one day return to that one for balance and transmutation. Thus, in the end every man does bear his own burden. When that day come, may the karmic task be accomplished in the joy of self-mastery and not with "weeping and gnashing of teeth."

The beautiful melody "None but the Lonely Heart" penetrates the corridors of our Ashram. But the words tell of a loneliness that comes to all through earth's most painful partings:

> None but the lonely heart knows of my sorrow;
> Alone and desolate I greet each morrow!
> I search the dawning sky a hope renewing
> Ah! What is life to me with thou departed!

> None but the lonely heart knows of my sorrow;
> Alone and desolate I greet each morrow,
> Alone, in separation; no joy, no gladness!
> My soul, though cold, with flame anew consumes me.
> None but the lonely heart could know my sorrow!

As I gaze with my spiritual eye from land to land the world around, I see millions of souls who are indeed "lonely hearts." Give these some thought sendings as you lovingly engage in our Ashram rituals and mantrams, that they might feel not alone but "all one" in God's Divine Love and be encouraged to pick up the pieces of their broken lives.

We are also reminded of the robins and the sparrows, the "common folk," for whom God cares:

> Said the Robin to the Sparrow:
> "I should really like to know
> Why these anxious human beings
> Rush about and worry so."

> Said the Sparrow to the Robin:
> "Friend, I think that it must be
> That they have no heavenly Father
> Such as cares for you and me."*

President Lincoln once had a dream in which he was at a party of common folk. One among them commented that the president himself was a "common-looking man." To this Lincoln replied: "Common-looking people are the best in the world: that is the reason the Lord makes so many of them."†

The so-called clay from which the Potter molded all life is one. Likewise the Father's design for his own is one. It is but the misuse of God's will by his children and their misappropriation of his gift of free will that has caused the atoms and molecules of their four lower bodies to be so enclosed with the shadows of a resultant

---

*Elizabeth Cheney, "Overheard in an Orchard."
†*Letters of John Hay and Extracts from His Diary*, December 23, 1863.

karma as to outpicture a warp and a twist in mind and form and feeling.

These distortions and disfigurings are prevalent on earth in the physical and astral planes, but they are not always recognized by either therapists or laymen, for they are often hidden in the recesses of the psyche at subconscious or unconscious levels; nevertheless, it is just such torques that rob life of its beauty and happiness.

It is true that human loneliness results from the apparent separation between the soul and her God. People are never so lonely as when they are in the midst of a crowd. In time of personal crisis this feeling of aloneness can become terrifying until the soul turns to her God and cries out for help.

Aloneness is not the intent of the Father. Furthermore, it is not real but always illusory. For Christ said, "I and my Father are one"; and in the Lord's Prayer he said, "*Our* Father," showing the common heritage and the common access of all of God's children to one another through their heavenly Father.

It follows, then, that the sense of aloneness is the karma of one's self-separation from the presence of the LORD through sin or the sense of sin. The soul who feels unworthy to stand in the presence of her LORD must seek restoration through repentance and the remission of her sin. She must seek and find self-worth in Christ and by his grace be an overcomer in all things that have separated her from the love of God in Christ Jesus.

The soul who would be reunited in God through the oneness of Father and Son must literally storm the citadels of heaven with her prayers for the Holy Spirit's violet flame transmutation of all her transgressions of the Law. Then she must invoke the strong right arm of Michael the Archangel to strengthen her in her resolve to "go and sin no more."

May you, the chelas of our Ashram, also storm the citadels of heaven with your invocations for comfort, consolation, wholeness and healing Truth as you offer your rituals this week on behalf of God's children who identify themselves as the lonely hearts of our world.

If you will call to Archangel Raphael and Mother Mary and their healing angels to heal the lonely hearts, heaven will answer your call without fail. And if you will call for the Spirit of the Lord GOD to come upon you, and the LORD, your Mighty I AM Presence, to anoint you, it shall be granted unto you according to your karma of good words and works and the stature of your Christhood. And the Holy Spirit may work a mighty work through you in your day even as he did through Jesus Christ.

Then you may go forth from our Ashram wearing the mantle of your devotions offered at our altar. Then you will rejoice with Isaiah, and his words will ring true in your heart:

The LORD hath anointed me to preach good tidings unto the meek; he hath sent me to bind up the brokenhearted, to proclaim liberty to the captives, and the opening of the prison to them that are bound;

To proclaim the acceptable year of the LORD, and the day of vengeance of our God; to comfort all that mourn;

To appoint unto them that mourn in Zion, to give unto them beauty for ashes, the oil of joy for mourning, the garment of praise for the spirit of heaviness; that they might be called trees of righteousness, the planting of the LORD, that he might be glorified.

And because you shall have submitted to Christ in all things, putting all things beneath his feet, many people will know the comfort of your God. And your rituals given regularly without fail will sustain them as they go through the sometimes painful, sometimes frightening process of reconnecting with their God Presence. And Divine Love continuously invoked by you in their behalf will break up and transmute the misqualified shadowy substance they have layered between themselves and their God.

As we enter the season when devotees of Christ may take the Lord's resurrection spiral and wrap it about themselves twice round from head to toe as a cloak, I send forth the call from the Ashram of God's Will here in Darjeeling to all my chelas to recite daily the mantram:

I AM the Resurrection and the Life
of my entire consciousness, being and world!

As is the case with all of the mantrams I have given you in the Notes and rituals, for best results you are instructed to recite it 9 times or in multiples of 27 up to 108. When you give this "I AM" mantram, you are affirming God's I AM Presence where you are, as the Resurrection and the Life of your entire consciousness, being and world.

Truly, miracles can and do happen when you recite the full cup of 108 mantrams. Feel free to use prayer beads to count them. Rudraksha beads are commonly used for this purpose in India.

As you invoke Christ's mantle of the Resurrection and the Life upon yourself, you will be able to multiply it by the power of your own Christ Self, Jesus working with you, and transfer it to all children of the Light on earth. For your Christ Self, with Jesus Christ, does have the power to multiply infinitely whatsoever of God-Good you can precipitate in Light as a gift of Love from your heart to all who are worthy who have need.

This is why Jesus promised: "He that believeth on me, the works that I do shall he do also; and greater works than these shall he do, because I go unto my Father."

As you engage in this Eastertide endeavor, you will be joined by Ascended Masters, unascended adepts, angel devas and my most advanced chelas, who work not only seasonally with the sacred fire of the Resurrection but also regularly with the Light of God's goodwill.

The aim of these servants of God, as they serve with the Brothers of the Diamond Heart, is to see to it that the flame of God's will is blazing within every heart; this is subject, of course, to the free will of the individual.

It is therefore our fiat that the Mystical Body of God, one in heaven and on earth, be charged with the Light of God's will, fully prepared to receive Resurrection's Flame on Easter morning.

May I suggest that you put your favorite picture or statue of Mary, the Mother of Jesus, on your altar.

Meditate on and offer your prayers and mantrams to her Immaculate Heart. Take all of your problems to her Immaculate Heart, and you will see that she will not fail you as long as you do not fail her. For so states the Law.

Remember, the Blessed Virgin holds the immaculate concept of Life's beauty and intended perfection on behalf of all of God's children until one by one they return to the glory they knew with the Father in the Beginning before the world was.

Bear in mind that if you were to live in my Ashram community at Darjeeling, you would be required to respect and fulfill my directives, even as the monks and nuns of holy orders respect the enforcement of the rules by their superiors.

Therefore I make you a promise: If you accept my words, both hearing and doing them, released through my Ashram Notes, having faith in God and in the power he has given me to transmit these words to you through my amanuensis; and further, if you will take my advice when it is given and follow my directives, thus being diligent in keeping the rituals and thereby tuning in to and even eventually embodying the vibration of my Electronic Presence; and if you are able to sustain the ray of Light from my heart to yours and send it back again, then regardless of how difficult such a feat may seem to the outer mind (which is always inclined to doubt, dear hearts), you shall most assuredly receive no less benefit from our association than do my disciples who live under my Ashram roof. And I do invite you to journey in your finer bodies to my etheric retreat escorted by my angels, as you are able.

Only by your failure to do your part in this grand equation can you be deprived of this the greatest blessing that can come to those evolving on planet earth—contact with Hierarchy.

This is a serious commitment that I am making to each chela who will meet me halfway with a like commitment.

Be free. Know the Good of the All and know that the All is in the all. Dare to know the Truth, to do the Truth and to work the works of Christ-Truth. Dare to work for Christ's glory in all and then to be silent, that the planted seed of Truth may grow and manifest that glory in the resurrection of a living soul!

Yours in hope,

El Morya

For your faithful prayers, invocations and loving cooperation we thank you. For sustaining this labor we thank you. May your Light increase. As you give, you shall receive. God bless you.

The Ashram Staff

March 2, 1958

38

Ashram Notes

Beloved, I joyously stand aside that Saint Germain may deliver his message to you.

I am turning more and more of the glory of my ray upon the people of earth. The longing in the hearts of God's people for true freedom has not slackened, nor has my endeavor to keep the freedom flame burning on all fronts.

Never have the events of earth proved more challenging, and never have the possibilities for total victory or total defeat been so present. Hope for social justice to all waits in the portal of free will while the juggernaut of science rolls on.

Yet, it remains for the lens of human perception to interpret passing events. Some choose to magnify out of all proportion the unimportant, all the while minimizing the urgent affairs of the Brotherhood. This is an avoidance technique employed by all who, in their rebellion against God, refuse to deal with reality.

Others, God be thanked, are content to put their faith in our endeavors, trusting our foresight and forewarnings of "things which must shortly come to pass," mindful of the Spirit and disregarding of any apparent flaw in our human representatives that might bubble to the surface.

I assure you that our cosmic achievements of past ages and other worlds were not built on flaws but on the flawless art of the adepts. We focused our attention on the goal and its perfect precipitation from the inner pattern to the physical manifestation. And we accomplished it!

The Law of Life decrees that the eye be single and the plan be submitted to the Solar Logoi. Once approved, the builders, with attention focused on the geometry of the design, may begin to build the matrix for the lowering into form of that structure that will contain the higher harmonies by its mathematical keys.

Thus the adepts knew the laws of fohat and built their temples to capture in Matter, by the angles of their architecture and the special building materials they used, the frequencies of Spirit. Their goal was to unite heaven and earth through an engineering not known on earth today. And this they accomplished in the more advanced civilizations of Atlantis and Lemuria. Their feats have not been equaled since, though vestiges remain, such as the pyramids.

For starts, I suggest you prove the law that says you will outpicture whatever you focus your attention on. Had we ourselves in our past incarnations set our attention on the appearance world, we would have become it. And we never would have achieved the God-mastery that we embody today.

You can see, I am sure, that although we Ascended Masters are free as we direct the Seventh Ray of freedom to all who by their devotion to freedom are able to carry its ray, we are dependent on each recipient's constructive use of free will.

Thus by the enlightened, responsible use of our ray, you can become ourselves in action in the world. As our hands and feet, you can extend the borders of the kingdom of God into the world of men that is seething with turbulence. And through you we will calm the storms, bringing God-dominion to loving hearts.

People from every walk of life need an angel in embodiment, "in the flesh," to hold the balance for them (until they are able to hold it for themselves) and to strengthen them in right decision and in the follow-through to right action to its completion.

Blessed hearts, we have won our freedom! While we were in the world, we were the Light (i.e., the Christ Presence) of the world, as Jesus said, but we are no longer of the physical plane.

Jesus passed the torch to you when he told you: "Ye are the Light of the world." It is up to unascended beings such as you, who appreciate the value of contact with Hierarchy and can accept your calling to be Christed ones, to unite in the cooperative endeavor of this worldwide Ashram.

Now is the hour to seal your Christhood, to internalize it and to consciously direct your free will in alignment with God's perfect plan. Go not after the false chelas who allow their energies to flow willy-nilly into the turbulent astral river of psychic probings, which acts to divert the human race from finding God in the name of avant-garde religion.

As earthly skies reflect the inner turmoil and torment of men's emotions and froward wills, they take on a leaden, or laden, appearance. Thus does

Nature relieve herself of the destructive potential of man's sowings, giving vent in driving storms, tornadoes, hurricanes and ultimately cataclysmic earth changes to the pent-up violence of the uncontrolled human consciousness at odds with the Deity.

The blue skies of goodwill are temporarily overcast by the din of a dissonant ill will. But the cause of all of mankind's misery can be traced back to their out-of-alignment state. They are out of line, and out of line with God's will. They defy the laws of God "written in their inward parts," recorded in every living cell from the foundation of the world.

The laws of God are summed up in the Love of Christ, who charged his disciples: "That ye love one another as I have loved you." Truly, Christ love is the healing of pride and rebellion and revenge—but only in those for whom Christ's love takes precedence over their pride, their rebellion and their revenge.

My stalwart co-worker, El Morya, expounding upon the teachings of Gautama Buddha on human suffering, has often hinted at this. For he works to sow the seeds of goodwill in all hearts, even as I work to transmute by the violet fire of pure Christ love the self-imposed darkness of mankind's wrong sowing, as they have blindly followed blind leaders as these have sowed the seeds of evil.

If my words seem repetitious, bear in mind that "Good! Good! Good!" repeated often (for it is in fact the name of God) is the pronouncement of God's approval of his creation in you and of your good works rendered in his name. Its repetition is harmless, thought-provoking and self-generating of God's Good within you.

Its opposite, "Bad! Bad! Bad!" spoken as a pronouncement of disapproval upon oneself or one's children or even one's animals is a damnable condemnation; it is a cursing of their persons, their souls and of elemental life. It can be subtle, as a disparagement of their words or their works, but the smarting sting of the sorrow or pain inflicted will be no less.

Even while I write, the children of Darkness do not cease their sowing of seeds of discord among the brethren of Light; their invectives and their judgments may leave scars in the psyche, but fear not, the violet flame will consume the strength of their sin against the brethren in all who love Christ's Love more.

The forces whose day is nearly done on this planet have marshaled their troops to engage the Light-bearers in a spiritual battle of Armageddon. This war of wars threatens to engulf the many tiny points of Light that make up our spiritual focuses across the planet and to divide the very souls whom we are striving to unite.

A spiritual warfare of souls is already being waged in the churches, synagogues, temples, mosques and spiritual orders of the whole world. Strife among the brethren is rampant, for by the division in their members they fall prey to the divisive tactics of devils discarnate and incarnate.

Therefore I am calling upon the members of our Ashram to hold a firm candle as you keep the flame of unity for the unascended brethren in your daily rituals, mantrams and meditations. I ask you to revive your faith and theirs in the Light of the Son of God within all who are of God, in the midst of a planetary Darkness that can only get darker unless the Light-bearers take dominion over their Christhood and become the Light of the world.

Do not be discouraged, for we are watching and attending the efforts of every struggling soul who seeks the Light. Practice faith in the Presence of God within you and within your neighbor, as beloved Jesus said. Practice hope and charity in offering calls at your altar to the Father-Mother God for the protection and the perfecting of the souls who are called to bring in God's kingdom on earth in the golden age to come.

Keep the waves of God peace flowing from your solar plexus to all children of the Light who sleep and must be awakened to the urgency of the hour that to them does not seem urgent. That they might arrive safely to the other shore is our mightiest prayer.

The cornucopia of heaven pours out its abundant Life into the worlds of my heart-friends of the ages as well as into the worlds of the sons of Light who will join them in calling forth the Seventh Ray and its violet flame of freedom. Let it be directed to all who apply its bountiful benefits with sobriety and respect for the Will of God, understanding that their day-to-day choices are exercised not only by the grace of God's gift of free will but by the foundations of freedom that were laid under my sponsorship in the Declaration of Independence and the Constitution of the United States of America.

This is the same Spirit of Freedom that made possible the raising of the Christ from the garden tomb and brought him to his release on Bethany's hill.

Have you ever thought about what freedom really means? No one can be truly free until he is free from the miscreations of his own mind. For he walls himself in with these mental stones of stumbling in a prison house more impervious than the human consciousness itself—because it is composed of the accumulated energy of his own lifestream and the building blocks of his airtight belief system.

And the veil of deception with which the carnal mind has covered the face of the soul is a veil of self-deception.

That the soul be not deceived, she must destroy the not-self before it destroys her. Only her purity in the love of God can deliver her from the carnal mind.

I quote the words of Paul that he wrote to the Christians in Rome. The message was given to him directly from the heart of Jesus and cannot be better said:

> For they that are after the flesh do mind the things of the flesh; but they that are after the Spirit the things of the Spirit.
>
> For to be carnally minded is death; but to be spiritually minded is life and peace.
>
> Because the carnal mind is enmity against God: for it is not subject to the law of God, neither indeed can be.
>
> So then they that are in the flesh cannot please God.
>
> But ye are not in the flesh, but in the Spirit, if so be that the Spirit of God dwell in you. Now if any man have not the Spirit of Christ, he is none of his.
>
> And if Christ be in you, the body is dead because of sin; but the Spirit is life because of righteousness.

But if the Spirit of him that raised up Jesus from the dead dwell in you, he that raised up Christ from the dead shall also quicken your mortal bodies by his Spirit that dwelleth in you.

Therefore, brethren, we are debtors, not to the flesh, to live after the flesh.

For if ye live after the flesh, ye shall die: but if ye through the Spirit do mortify the deeds of the body, ye shall live.

To rend in twain the veil woven out of the carnal mind's enmity with Christ and the fleshly consciousness that that mind has put on the soul as a death shroud is my goal. The flame of freedom will consume all enmity of the not-self against God and his Christ. Just call to me daily without fail to saturate your soul with the violet flame, and give it even one-tenth the effort you put into forming the attractions of the flesh.

May the freedom flame of the I AM THAT I AM that blazed before Moses in the bush that burned but was not consumed, and later carved out the law on tablets of stone in the Sinai wilderness, continue to blaze a trail to the new age of spiritual freedom—even as it was the zeal in my heart when as Columbus I sailed the *Santa Maria* to the New World and when I stood in Independence Hall July 4, 1776, to catalyze the patriots to "Sign that document!" for the freedom of all mankind.

I AM pinning *my* faith, *my* hope and *my* charity on endeavors like Morya's Ashram, knowing as I do your hearts' longing to meet your God face to face, and your hearts' understanding that to work a work for the Great White Brotherhood in this age is the surest way to that goal.

May you thank God every day that Morya has provided you with the means: a path of service that is daily rewarded by the Master's tutoring and testing of your souls.

Be comforted by the Light upon the hill that shall not be hid. For it is your Light, one in and as the Ashram. And always remember that your Saviour has said, "Ye are the Light of the World." And in so saying the Lord gave your souls a fiat for the Piscean age.

We are here to help you fulfill his mandate to you. So keep that freedom flame burning! burning! burning! and never let it go out in the hope! hope! hope! of our common cause:

God-freedom for every lifestream who has descended from the Great Central Sun and for every living soul upon this blessed planet who remains in the service of the Ancient of Days!

I AM ever thyself,
Saint Germain

Eternal remembrances,

El Morya

April 6, 1958

39

Ashram Notes

Dearly Beloved,

As such I greet you, for it is unthinkable that my regard for you should be otherwise, from the least in the chain of Hierarchy upward.

Truly it is my wish that you should feel such tenderness toward all children of the Light, no matter how far they have strayed from our Father's heart. For in their hearts his flame yet burns. And in his flame is the Divine Image of Alpha himself.

The harmony you express as you work with those who love the things of our realm is of heaven itself, and the energy of such cooperation qualified by the power of Love becomes eternal in those who hold on to it.

I need not remind, for you know the law: energy poured out in human nonsense is wasted energy. When you enter in to the whiling away of the hours in the purposeless pursuits of those wayward children who have not yet come into the Light as you have, instead of setting the example of the higher way of living life purposefully, you fall back to their level and make a heap of karma for yourself—because you know better.

For unto whomsoever much is given, of him shall be much required: and to whom men have committed much, of him they will ask the more.

Events of import to the children of earth gather like dark clouds, for the dangers of military conflict have waxed hot in recent weeks. I call upon you who have proven trustworthy in the past to pour out your prayers to the Lords of Karma and the ascended host to charge the quality of Cosmic Christ Peace into the vortex of all potential conflict, thus changing its momentum from world war to world peace.

Of these days Jesus prophesied:

And when ye shall hear of wars and rumours of wars, be ye not troubled: for such things must needs be; but the end shall not be yet.

The karmic portent for war on a planetary scale is there, written in akasha,* for the closing decades of the century. Only those who act in time to resolve all conflict in the psyche will be able to hold the balance of peace for the planet when the karma of the nations falls due:

For nation shall rise against nation, and kingdom against kingdom: and there shall be earthquakes in divers places, and there shall be famines and troubles: these are the beginnings of sorrows . . . .

*akasha [Sanskrit, from the root kāś, meaning "to be visible, appear," "to shine brightly," "to see clearly"]: primary substance; the subtlest, ethereal essence, which fills the whole of space; "etheric" energy vibrating at a certain frequency so as to absorb, or record, all of the impressions of life.

But when ye shall see the abomination of desolation, spoken of by Daniel the prophet, standing where it ought not (let him that readeth understand), then let them that be in Judaea flee to the mountains:

And let him that is on the housetop not go down into the house, neither enter therein, to take any thing out of his house . . . .

For in those days shall be affliction, such as was not from the beginning of the creation which God created unto this time, neither shall be.

And except that the Lord had shortened those days, no flesh should be saved: but for the elect's sake, whom he hath chosen, he hath shortened the days . . . .

But in those days, after that tribulation, the sun shall be darkened, and the moon shall not give her light,

And the stars of heaven shall fall, and the powers that are in heaven shall be shaken . . . .

Heaven and earth shall pass away: but my words shall not pass away.

But of that day and that hour knoweth no man, no, not the angels which are in heaven, neither the Son, but the Father.

Only by seeking God's peace in all that you do will you find the path to our abode. We are not so far from you and often pass among you unnoticed because at times your thoughts have, alas, an earthly vibration that is less than peaceful and far from the Peace-commanding Presence of our Saviour Jesus Christ.

You cannot be the instruments for "Peace on earth, goodwill to men" as long as there is a warring in your members.

Paul described what it is like to be in bondage to the law of karma, to sin and the struggle against sin, until there is the redemption of the soul through Jesus Christ and the lawful balancing of one's karma through the baptism by the sacred fire of the Holy Ghost, which consumes the cause, effect, record and memory of karma through a life of holiness in submission to God:

> For that which I do I allow not: for what I would, that do I not; but what I hate, that do I.
>
> If then I do that which I would not, I consent unto the law that it is good.
>
> Now then it is no more I that do it, but sin that dwelleth in me.
>
> For I know that in me (that is, in my flesh) dwelleth no good thing: for to will is present with me; but how to perform that which is good I find not.
>
> For the good that I would I do not: but the evil which I would not, that I do.
>
> Now if I do that I would not, it is no more I that do it, but sin that dwelleth in me.
>
> I find then a law, that, when I would do good, evil is present with me.
>
> For I delight in the law of God after the inward man:
>
> But I see another law in my members, warring against the law of my mind, and bringing me into captivity to the law of sin which is in my members.

O wretched man that I am! who shall
deliver me from the body of this death?

Afterwards liberated through his heart's oneness with the flaming grace of Jesus Christ, Paul
exclaimed:

I thank God through Jesus Christ our
Lord. So then with the mind I myself serve the
law of God; but with the flesh the law of sin.

There is therefore now no condemnation
to them which are in Christ Jesus, who walk not
after the flesh, but after the Spirit.

For the law of the Spirit of life in Christ
Jesus hath made me free from the law of sin
and death.

Remember, you need not forsake joy to find us
and the Father of all Life. You need only forsake
sorrows, exchanging them for eternal joy as you labor
a labor of Love unceasing day or night.

Strive harder to reach our circle—peacefully.
I long to begin the process of initiating the worthy!
Morya awaits.

I AM yours,

Morya El

August 1, 1958

Heart, Head and Hand Decrees
by El Morya

Violet Fire

Heart
   Violet Fire, thou Love divine,
   Blaze within this heart of mine!
   Thou art Mercy forever true,
   Keep me always in tune with you.

Head
   I AM Light, thou Christ in me,
   Set my mind forever free;
   Violet Fire, forever shine
   Deep within this mind of mine.

   God who gives my daily bread,
   With Violet Fire fill my head
   Till thy radiance heavenlike
   Makes my mind a mind of Light.

Hand
   I AM the hand of God in action,
   Gaining Victory every day;
   My pure soul's great satisfaction
   Is to walk the Middle Way.

Tube of Light

Beloved I AM Presence bright,
Round me seal your Tube of Light
From Ascended Master flame
Called forth now in God's own name.
Let it keep my temple free
From all discord sent to me.

I AM calling forth Violet Fire
To blaze and transmute all desire,
Keeping on in Freedom's name
Till I AM one with the Violet Flame.

Forgiveness

I AM Forgiveness acting here,
Casting out all doubt and fear,
Setting men forever free
With wings of cosmic Victory.

I AM calling in full power
For Forgiveness every hour;
To all life in every place
I flood forth forgiving Grace.

Supply

I AM free from fear and doubt,
Casting want and misery out,
Knowing now all good Supply
Ever comes from realms on high.

I AM the hand of God's own Fortune
Flooding forth the treasures of Light,
Now receiving full Abundance
To supply each need of Life.

Perfection

I AM Life of God-Direction,
Blaze thy light of Truth in me.
Focus here all God's Perfection,
From all discord set me free.

Make and keep me anchored ever
In the Justice of thy plan—
I AM the Presence of Perfection
Living the Life of God in man!

Transfiguration

I AM changing all my garments,
Old ones for the bright new day;
With the Sun of Understanding
I AM shining all the way.

I AM Light within, without;
I AM Light is all about.
Fill me, free me, glorify me!
Seal me, heal me, purify me!
Until transfigured they describe me:
I AM shining like the Son,
I AM shining like the Sun!

Resurrection

I AM the Flame of Resurrection
Blazing God's pure Light through me.
Now I AM raising every atom,
From every shadow I AM free.

I AM the Light of God's full Presence,
I AM living ever free.
Now the flame of Life eternal
Rises up to Victory. (3x)

Ascension

I AM Ascension Light,
Victory flowing free,
All of Good won at last
For all eternity.

I AM Light, all weights are gone.
Into the air I raise;
To all I pour with full God Power
My wondrous song of praise.

All hail! I AM the living Christ,
The ever-loving One.
Ascended now with full God Power,
I AM a blazing Sun! (3x)

Gratitude to Our Master Morya
From the Chela to the Guru

Master Morya, we thank you for all that you do
In the raising of mankind of earth
Blazing forth your light rays through the hearts of the few
Dedicating their souls to new birth.

Let us ever draw forth from the Presence above
The Light that illumines all men
So they see the good works of the Father of Love
And the Masters walk with us again.

Master Morya, our hearts are o'erflowing with love
For the Light and the Truth that you bring
Teach us ever to live in the Presence above
That through us the angels may sing.

Let us all understand and ever expand
The knowledge of God's sacred fire
That the earth may be raised to her place in the Sun
In fulfillment of your great desire.

Master Morya, we bless thee for being the one
To assist our belov'd Saint Germain
To expand his great work as before thou hast done
And to raise us again and again.

Thou art always adored, thou Great Cosmic Lord
Now step through the veil to our sight
That we all may be bathed in the Light from thy heart
Dedicated as guardians of Light.

Melody: a ballad by Thomas Moore, "Believe Me, If All Those Endearing Young Charms"

I AM God's Will
by El Morya

In the name of the beloved Mighty Victorious Presence of God I AM in me, and my own beloved Holy Christ Self, I call to the heart of the Will of God in the Great Central Sun, beloved Archangel Michael, beloved El Morya, beloved Mighty Hercules, all the legions of blue lightning and the Brothers of the Diamond Heart, beloved Lanello, the entire Spirit of the Great White Brotherhood and the World Mother, elemental life—fire, air, water, and earth! to fan the flame of the Will of God throughout my four lower bodies and answer this my call infinitely, presently, and forever:

1. I AM God's Will manifest everywhere,
   I AM God's Will perfect beyond compare,
   I AM God's Will so beautiful and fair,
   I AM God's willing bounty everywhere.

Refrain:
   Come, come, come, O blue-flame Will so true,
   Make and keep me ever radiant like you.
   Blue-flame Will of living Truth,
   Good Will flame of eternal youth,
   Manifest, manifest, manifest in me now!

2. I AM God's Will now taking full command,
   I AM God's Will making all to understand,
   I AM God's Will whose power is supreme,
   I AM God's Will fulfilling heaven's dream.

3. I AM God's Will protecting, blessing here,
   I AM God's Will now casting out all fear,
   I AM God's Will in action here well done,
   I AM God's Will with Victory for each one.

4. I AM blue lightning flashing Freedom's love,
   I AM blue-lightning power from above,
   I AM blue lightning setting all men free,
   I AM blue-flame power flowing good through me.

And in full Faith I consciously accept this manifest, manifest, manifest! (3x) right here and now with full Power, eternally sustained, all-powerfully active, ever expanding, and world enfolding until all are wholly ascended in the Light and free!

Beloved I AM! Beloved I AM! Beloved I AM!

THE SUMMIT LIGHTHOUSE
A World Pillar

Have you ever asked yourself, "Why am I me and not another? Am I different from others? What makes me unique?"

Do you remember your thoughts as a child when you dreamed about the great "work-a-day world" and longed to grow up to be a part of adult life? Perhaps you wanted to be a farmer, a teacher, a policeman, a scientist or an astronaut.

Do you now find that life has provided you with the happiness you then expected? Or are you searching for something beyond those childhood ambitions—something to fill the void that remained after worldly pursuits were attained?

The familiar image of Atlas holding up the earth and the heavens evokes the question of your own contribution to the total world structure: Have you considered how much your thoughts and acts influence the rest of life? Have you been able to realize your desire to add to and preserve the world's heritage of good? Are you a World Pillar?

The few enlightened ones in every age used their skills to build civilization as we know it today. They stood as World Pillars. What would be the outcome if tomorrow the *many* were to take up that calling to stand as World Pillars? What if they were given that "know-how" and decided to develop and exercise it in order to perfect the superstructure? If the many were to take up the objectives of peace and goodwill as building blocks, would we see more substantial and progressive change upon the world scene?

Your present outlook is made up of what you have retained from past experiences and learning. But your future remains unborn. It awaits new impressions you will form and nobler purposes wedded to more positive action that you will create consciously, willingly and hopefully.

Are you prepared to strive for the noble achievement deserving of God's love and worthy of man, made in his image? Or will you float in the uncharted rapids of mediocrity?

Have today's halls of learning met your needs? Did your parents and teachers impart to you the knowledge of wisdom's rod and a golden-rule blueprint for living, instilling in you reverence for all life and the joy of being your brother's keeper?

Does greater happiness lie in a more profound understanding of life's meaning than that which is given in the surface knowledge of science, law, culture, religion and psychology?

Is there one true religion and are all others false? Can God be known only through creed or rote? And does he confine himself to one faith alone?

An approach to these challenging questions and many more is available for your personal examination through the teachings of the Great White Brotherhood, published by The Summit Lighthouse.

You can mold your life in more constructive patterns through the application of inner laws that have been guarded by the elect for thousands of years.

They are revealed today by the Ascended Masters to hearts waiting to fulfill their destiny in the universal scheme and to minds unprejudiced by custom or fear.

The Great White Brotherhood is a spiritual fraternity to which beloved Jesus the Christ, Gautama Buddha, Confucius, Zarathustra, Mother Mary, the Apostle Paul, Saint Germain, El Morya and many other great avatars, saints and sages of all ages belong. The term "white" refers not to race but to the aura of white light that surrounds these immortals.

This organization of Ascended Masters disseminates Truth to the world through The Summit Lighthouse, an arm of the Brotherhood that is free from commercialization and dedicated to the expansion of light, love and perfection in man and society.

This "outer" World Pillar of the "inner" (spiritual) hierarchy works to implement a victorious fulfillment for all of God's people by making plain the path of the ascension of the Christ consciousness in each individual. The Teachings of the Ascended Masters, unadulterated by mere human concepts and theorizing, are cups of radiant Light, illumination, healing, comfort and courage to all who partake of them.

The Summit Lighthouse is an activity born of hope for a better world made ready to receive the blessings of the incoming golden age through the application of greater wisdom. Its members strive to use the eternal Light and Truth, expressed so ably in the past by the many great teachers and prophets, as stepping stones into greater spiritual progress, knowing that much yet remains to be revealed to mankind.

Members of The Summit Lighthouse believe in "home rule," which maintains individual and national independence in perfect balance with social and national interdependence of man with man and nation with nation. They understand the necessity for individuals and nations to assume the responsibilities of self-government as the foundation for equitable world government and genuine world brotherhood.

No man, organization or nation is an island; neither can all be grouped in one mainland. In becoming interdependent, men and nations must not surrender their individuality. Each element should complement the other by imparting to and receiving manifold blessings from the whole, thereby completing the divine design.

A "Summiteer" seeks the best in self, self-government and religion, advocating harmonious cooperation among all peoples, nations and faiths through such "home rule" as will make each nation, planet and star "Home Sweet Home."

The function of The Summit Lighthouse is to promulgate progressive truth and a greater understanding of universal law through teachings released by the Ascended Masters. It is their supreme endeavor to make practical for humanity's needs that Law which is the irrevocable will of God, molded by Love and shaped by Wisdom's hand.

For, in truth, the Law gives freedom from all oppression to those who apply it and renders hearts receptive to the voice from on high that speaks to every man, woman and child, saying, "Lo, I AM come that ye might have Life, and that more abundantly!"

In teaching the science of universal law, the Ascended Masters seek to instill the love of virtue and perfection in every heart and home in order to bring men nearer to God, their own Christ identity and their brethren. Thus their future joys and accomplishments for the world order will exceed past attainments—even as the brilliance of the sun contrasts with the light of a penny candle.

The grace and uplifting peace of the Ascended Masters is radiated out daily from the Summit Beacon, reaching their immediate circle of chelas (disciples), who, in turn, focus these energies for all of God's people on earth. The Summit Lighthouse World Pillar is the forerunner of the spiritual ideal of perfection that is attainable here and now by each one through the direct assistance of his individualized God Presence and the host of Ascended Masters.

The Truth enshrined in The Summit Lighthouse, then, is the science of attaining the summit of being—the highest good in man, which is God. Like a tiny acorn, this kernel of Truth expands to become the towering oak from which can be hewn, in a labor of Universal Love, a Temple of Victory dedicated to the glorification of God in all life.

The Ascended Masters reach the consciousness of their students through many avenues, but none more direct than the weekly letters called *Pearls of Wisdom*. If you choose to study these releases from week to week, you will find your soul renewed by the gentle impartations of love from your "friends of Light." All are welcome to receive *Pearls of Wisdom*, especially those who, through greater attunement with the divine spark within them, yearn to be World Pillars.

If you are interested in securing more advanced instruction, you may wish to inquire about the Keepers of the Flame Fraternity, whose members are dedicated to the freedom and enlightenment of humanity and to keeping the greater Light of Life, Wisdom and Love burning in the lamp of being. Members receive periodic lessons written by the ascended hierarchy, which contain teaching on the Law ranging from the most basic principles to deeper concepts formerly given only to initiates in the retreats of the Great White Brotherhood.

Greater understanding of our common source can help us all to find our way "Home." Receive, then, if you will, the circle of concentrated illumination emanating from the high tower of The Summit, built upon the rock of divine Truth.

We remind all that there is a summit of divine identity within everyone—whether they are consciously aware of that guiding Presence or only suspect it—and that there is a summit of victorious achievement of highest purpose for the earth that men must one day realize, individually and collectively, in order to bring in the great golden age at the appointed hour.

As Diogenes walked the streets with his lantern in search of an honest heart, so we bid you to join us in your search for the nobility that you know to be your true self. For that quest and that Grail is as much yours as any man's.

Write today to The Summit Lighthouse and request *Pearls of Wisdom* on a free-will, love-offering basis, and information on the Keepers of the Flame Fraternity.

We bid you welcome to the road of victorious achievement and the opportunity to one day be able to say, "I AM a World Pillar."

THE UNIVERSAL ASHRAM
OF DEVOTEES OF THE WILL OF GOD

*Contact with the Brotherhood
through the Ashram Ritual-Meditations*

Excerpts from a dictation by El Morya
through the Messenger Elizabeth Clare Prophet

———

O Chela of the Will of God:

Here with you in full presence, yet also in Darjeeling, I am the Diamond Heart of this movement. . . .

I am present in the midst of the eye of the hurricane, as are ye in the great manifestation of the will of God that is the vortex of light around this community. Thus, we are in the heart of the Ashram, for is not the Ashram the nucleus of all energy systems? Aye, indeed it is! . . .

The Ashram is ever present. It is a world order. There are many members outside of this community that has gathered around the original Summit Lighthouse who are my chelas. They uphold the Ashramic consciousness; and the antahkarana has been abuilding for thirty, forty years and more.

For the understanding of the Ashram as the house of Light, the dwelling place of the Guru and the chela, gives comfort to all. It is the comfort flame midst the storm. It is the light in the cabin window that is seen afar off by the traveler through the night storm.

The Ashram is the haven. It is the resting place. It is the special place that, wherever you find it, is the same as every other such place. Surcease from the struggle, entering in for the recharge, brothers and sisters of one mind and heart and purpose meeting here and there along life's way in our secluded out-posts—such is the vision of the Ashram that I hold and that does exist.

Therefore you, too, have been nestled in that place, which many have prepared by the stretching of the antahkarana of a cosmos. Feel now the thread of this antahkarana pass through your heart. It is truly a thread of Light.

And therefore, if you will tremble the thread by using at least one of the meditations daily (and there are indeed short ones that no one should find excuse to neglect), then you see, you will always be a part of the antahkarana. You will always be able to hear with the inner ear and hear with the heart what is the situation of all servitors of the will of God of a cosmos.

You stand to benefit much from this association; for admittedly many are beyond your attainment, some the unascended adepts, others Ascended Masters and Cosmic Beings. And therefore, you may deliver to those of lesser attainment their momentum even while you yourselves are strengthened by that impetus from above.

Indeed the Ashram is an impulse. It is an impulse to love and to fulfill the commands of Christ Jesus. We are worshipers of the universal manifestation of the Christ. Yet we are here to fulfill the words of the Saviour Jesus Christ, who is Lord and must be seen as Lord by those who would enter the heart of God's will and receive the strength to fulfill it; for without Christ ye cannot.

Shorn lambs, yes, karma-bearers, yes, and those who have vested no small amount of energy in other causes that are not of God's will. Therefore, until all of these strands be withdrawn from an investment unwise, you see, you require the intercessor in order to do the will of God. The intercessor is indeed the mantram, is indeed the meditation, is indeed the ritual! For I and my Father are one.[1]

And, lo, Christ will whisper to you, "I AM the Word and my Word is manifest in you as you allow that Word to resound through you." And so as you do, beloved, first you become the manifestation of the words of Christ, and then millions of words clustered together in a diamond heart become the chalice for the Word itself.

And one day you will know:

I, too, with Christ am the Word incarnate,
For there is no longer separation
    between me and my Lord.
For I AM one in his words.
I have drunk his Blood.
I have assimilated his Flesh.
And I am that I AM, *which He is,* where I am.

Lo, it is He!
Lo, He cometh!
Lo, He cometh where I AM in the Ashram
    or in the eye of the hurricane.
Lo, He cometh.
Ten thousand of his saints surround me.

And I AM One —
I AM One in Him and He in me
  by the Word incarnate.

Thus, the Ashram is indeed a means to an end, and that end is total identification with the Word of God. It is the strengthening of hearts that we seek, and ritual has evermore been the means to that end. The ritual itself does increase the capacity of the individual to hold mighty currents of energy. As the capacity does increase, you are transformed.

Rituals are self-transforming.

Listen as I give them with you through the Messenger. Listen to the quality of the voice of Lanello and of myself as you hear the fervor of love and realize that the Messenger is teaching you by example how to create a chalice for Light from the recitation of the Word.

The mere repetition of words will not suffice in this pursuit. Every word you speak, even as you hear me speaking now, is put forth with a power, with a fervor of adoration and gratitude to God. In fact, our spoken word does carry all of our being and the stamp of our individuality. So when you recite your rituals, may the sacred fire breath carry into your words the Light of your heart.

When these words are sent forth, there is no ending to them. They cross the Matter spheres and bless all Life. Such is the nature of the word of the Guru! Emulate this delivery, beloved, in your Ashram rituals so that your words, as cups of Light moving on a conveyor belt, shall reach millions of hearts of Light, never stopped by distance; for these words given in this fashion travel beyond ordinary wave-lengths of sound.

There is indeed the Light and Sound Ray whereby the words of the Guru are carried wherever in the universe the Guru is manifest as God. And they are shuttled across the skies from star to star, and all who are chelas of the will of God who have reached a certain level of attainment listen with the inner ear for the conveyances of the Word as Power, the Word as Teaching, the Word as Love, the Word as the exegesis on the Law itself and the scriptures of East and West.

Now understand how the Word of Jesus Christ does live forever beyond heaven and earth. For it is beyond these octaves that the Word goes coursing on its way, nourishing Life and holding the balance of the universal Ashram of the devotees of the will of God.

Blessed ones, all who have any level of attainment whatsoever must be devotees of the will of God. Thus, you begin to see the magnitude of our Ashram, that the entire Spirit of the Great White Brotherhood is a part of the antahkarana that you enter when with regular rhythmic cycle you recite our rituals.

In the beginning was the Word, indeed. And in the ending is the Word as the Work of the Lord. And in the middle is the Word. And everywhere is the Word!

Now then, beloved, I assure you that it would please me highly if you should seek out and find those souls of Light of a similar wavelength to your own to bring them the message of the universal Ashram of the Light of God's holy will, that they might understand

that by a little entering in and a little joy in the vibrations that pour through the worded release of our
meditations, they might find the true communion of
saints and oneness with all who have ever loved the
will of God.

This strengthening process is necessary. For
when you do not receive from the earth currents or
the earth itself its nutrients and all that you require
for the strength of the body and the mind, for clarity
of perception, for functioning in the capacity of an
unascended adept, as you are called to do, then I tell
you that the channels that you tie in to and reinforce
by your words in our meditations will open up to you
the energy and the currents of Light to make up the
difference against the problems of pollution of this
world or any other world so contaminated.

Our God does not leave you comfortless! Our
God can supply you with Light and equalize your
needs. But if the channels be not open, if they be not
sustained, beloved, then when you have need you are
not tied in to the Ashram. Moreover, through this
antahkarana you experience the direct tie to your
Mighty I AM Presence (when in the karmic state you
would not otherwise be able to sustain it), for you are
perpetually in touch with Cosmic Beings.

What of the decrees and the decree momentum
of many years? All of this does reinforce the rituals,
but the rituals are very special. They are very precious. They are foundational and fundamental to all
who would begin on the Path and run and not be
weary[2] and complete their course.

The ritual is the means of devotion, and
through this devotion and your application of the

instructions for visualization, you gain a certain skill by fervor of heart, by will of the mind and by caring for other parts of Life.

To send Light and to intensify the Light ray, as you see it shoot forth from your heart, you must visualize the intensification of it and direct it for all God-Good wherever the need is greatest. Thus, meditation will strengthen your vision and aid in the clearing of the third-eye chakra as you use it more and more to project only good to every part of God's Life.

The meditations are a dispensation. They come from the Causal Body of a great Cosmic Being who has also been my mentor. And through my heart this release to my chelas does complete a circle that can take you to far-off worlds that are the abode of this great being.

Thus, beloved, in all ways know that we have many reasons for which we do many things. And though I could speak to you for many an hour on the realities of the Ashram and what it can mean to your acceleration on the Path, I do request that as chelas of the will of God you will accept my word, that it is so.

Accept that this bonding together of your souls with one another, with my heart and with all servants of God's will is a major key in your success and your God-victory. This applies even in the matter of the initiation at the two-thirds level of the pyramid, even in the matter of the expansion of resurrection's flame in your heart, given to you with such love, such ineffable love, by Jesus.[3]

Yes, your participation in the Ashram ritual-meditations will strengthen you to accomplish all that you desire by a path of self-mastery.

Thus, let the community, let the chelas determine when they desire to group together to give these rituals. Let it be the spontaneous will of all. Let their votes be made known and suggestions filed. Thus, we may commune together in these rituals when it is the free, God-given gift of those who participate. May it be your link to the future and the arc whereby the soul may pass over the Dark Night of the nineties and be in place in the matrix of the will of God.

Trust me that you must be in the earth yet not of it. Conquer self. Establish right livelihood. And if you do not have it as a sufficiency in your life, know that inasmuch as it is one of the requirements of the Eightfold Path of the Buddha,* there is some force of the anti-Buddha within the self that you must go after. For right livelihood is the very nature of the Path itself, and wrong livelihood will not profit your soul nor be for the balancing of karma.

Thus, if greed or any other vice color your motive in livelihood, you will not be accelerating on the Path. Consider, then, the requirements of the Buddha on the Eightfold Path and bring your lives into proper adjustment. Unless you can call to the Five Dhyani Buddhas and earnestly desire the removal of the five poisons, unless you can call to Cyclopea for the vision to see what poisons bring ailments to the spirit and the soul and the mind, it is difficult for me to help you.

But when you are a part of the Ashram rituals, you receive pulsations of my mind and you enter into your own mind of Christ; and you see things in yourself that you don't like and you are strengthened to

*right understanding, right thought, right speech, right action, right livelihood, right effort, right mindfulness, right concentration.

deal with them. And you will not fall apart when you discover things about yourself that you have not been willing to look at before.

The abundant Life must be demonstrated by those who espouse the path of embodying virtue. Virtue does lead to the building of the magnet of the heart, and Love can only attract more of itself. And the magnet of Love does always bring all things necessary to the one who carries that magnet of Love to the exclusion of all lesser vibrations.

Now in the heart of the Mystery School I AM come. The thread of the antahkarana of the Ashram I have passed through your heart. Now I make this offer to you to establish a focus of the Ashram by giving the rituals and seeking to expand the circle of your meditation, inviting those who will come and those who would enter in.

If you establish this forcefield, even if you are alone in your home, if you establish a weekly routine of daily meditations and keep it, I, Morya, Lord of the First Ray, will sustain for you the matrix of the Ashram where you are. If possible, consecrate a place where you give your rituals and keep it holy. Even a little corner of a room will do.

Thus, beloved, the Ashram always has been and always will be without requirements except devotion. You do not need membership cards. You do not need written pledges or dues or anything else. You have the *Ashram Notes* to study and restudy.

There are souls in other dimensions who use this little book as a bible for their entering into the heart of the will of God. The *Notes* give impetus to profound meditation upon God and his Christ; they are like the bittersweet candy in the mouth that will never dissolve but always be there to savor again and again.

Thus, I, El Morya, with my chelas desire to bring to all whom we meet the Communion cup and morsel by morsel the bread of angels, *panis angelicus.* It is a piece[4] I love to hear again and again. Whenever you play it, I shall be there; for I love Jesus' sermon "I AM the bread of Life which came down from heaven."[5]

Truly Christ is the bread of Life, and one crumb of that loaf is able to transform a universe. And when one who does not know Christ Jesus comes to that point of love and profound knowing of the Master, all doors of a cosmos can be opened unto him.

Therefore, not in mountains of material but in the love quality of your heart will you find yourself being able to offer morsels of that bread of our Lord. And the wine of the Spirit each one shall drink in, for you cannot send forth the word of a ritual unto a cosmos without it returning to you the Light essence of your immortality to be.

In truth, with my amanuensis Mark Prophet I have opened a door to thousands and millions through the Ashramic consciousness. Now, beloved, I have passed the torch, I have given you the key. The book is in your hands. May you let it do the work, and may you be its handmaid and the handmaid delivering souls to worship their God and to be free to know Christ. . . .

The Ashram is the true introduction to The Summit Lighthouse, which is built on this foundation. May you now go about placing that foundation in your lives, for you will need it in the coming days and months....

I remind you of the pay-as-you-go policy of the Brotherhood. What you give us in the decrees offered in my name, we will multiply and send back to you. Give us the Light, the energy and the decree momentum. Increase your contact with the Brotherhood by the rituals, and you will see what Morya will do for each and every one of you. It is a pact we make with all who are true members by action of our Ashram.

We will not fail you, beloved. Give us the Light. Give us the energy. Give us the will. Give us the faith and trust, and listen with the inner ear to obey our voice. Then you shall see in full, grand display what the brothers in white are capable of on behalf of true chelas.

These are my thoughts in this hour, beloved. Watch and pray, that ye enter not into temptation, and watch the events of the world scene. No chela must ever be caught off guard when it comes to planetary events and cycles and his own personal life. You must be astute enough to anticipate the future by the signs of the times that you read and sense each and every day.

Thus, I AM with you. Thus, my Presence remains over my Messenger that you might contact me at a more physical level. And I am truly grateful for her service and staying power as well as for her compassionate heart, even as I am grateful to you for your faithfulness and your striving and your devotion and your presence that continually makes possible the activities of this Church and the service of the Messenger.

We of the Darjeeling Council salute you.
We encourage you!
And we say: Onward, chelas of the sacred fire!
Courage! Courage! Courage!

Royal Teton Ranch
July 8, 1990

(1) John 10:30. (2) Isa. 40:31. (3) See Jesus Christ, July 8, 1990, "The Gift of Resurrection's Flame," in 1990 *Pearls of Wisdom,* pp. 423–27. (4) "Panis Angelicus" by composer César Franck. (5) John 6:26–59.

The Ascended Master El Morya, Chief of the Darjeeling Council of the Great White Brotherhood, directed Mark L. Prophet to found The Summit Lighthouse in Washington, D.C., in August 1958 for the purpose of publishing the Teachings of the Ascended Masters.

The anointed Messengers Mark L. Prophet and Elizabeth Clare Prophet were trained by their Guru El Morya to receive the Word of the LORD in the form of both spoken and written dictations from the Ascended Masters. Since 1958, the personal instruction of the Masters to their chelas in every nation has been published in weekly letters called *Pearls of Wisdom.*

Before his ascension on February 26, 1973, Mark transferred the mantle of the mission to Elizabeth. Mrs. Prophet continues to set forth the mysteries of the Holy Grail in current *Pearls of Wisdom,* Keepers of the Flame Lessons, and at Summit University three-month retreats, weekend seminars and quarterly conferences.

These activities are headquartered at the Royal Teton Ranch, a 30,000-acre self-sufficient spiritual community-in-the-making adjacent to Yellowstone National Park in southwest Montana. They are sponsored by the Brotherhood as the foundation of the culture and religion of Aquarius.

For information on volumes of *Pearls of Wisdom* published since 1958 and numerous books and audio- and videocassettes distributed by The Summit Lighthouse, write for a free catalog.